Paradise by Design

Also by Kathryn Phillips

Tracking the Vanishing Frogs: An Ecological Mystery

Kathryn Phillips

Paradise by Design

Native Plants and the New American Landscape

North Point Press
Farrar, Straus and Giroux
New York

North Point Press
A division of Farrar, Straus and Giroux
19 Union Square West, New York 10003

Distributed in Canada by Douglas & McIntyre Ltd.
Printed in the United States of America
Designed by Jonathan D. Lippincott
First edition, 1998

Library of Congress Cataloging-in-Publication Data
Phillips, Kathryn.
Paradise by design : native plants and the new American landscape / Kathryn Phillips
p. cm.
ISBN 0-86547-519-9 (alk. paper)
1. Janecki, Joni. 2. Landscape architecture—United States. 3. Natural gardens, American—California—Montecito. 4. Native plants for cultivation—United States. 5. Landscape architects—California—Biography. I. Title.
SB470.J35P48 1998
712'.092—dc21
[B] 97-18172

To Charles W. Phillips

Paradise by Design

I

IF YOU ASK ABBE SANDS HOW SHE AND HER HUSband, Dennis, have managed over the years to complete herculean remodeling jobs on their homes, somewhere in the answer she'll bring up the "want" thing. The want thing is that bone-deep desire to achieve a goal. The want thing helps inspire you not to give up when a project gets tough. The want thing means not letting time get in the way, not feeling pressured by deadlines. It means persevering and, when the situation gets overwhelming, bringing in an expert for help.

On a cloudless August day, Abbe steers her forest-green Range Rover onto the freeway off-ramp and toward home. The want thing is at work. In the passenger seat beside her is Joni Janecki, a landscape architect who has flown in from Santa Cruz, California, a funky beachside university town eighty-five miles south of San Francisco. She is here to spend a day at the Sands' home in Montecito, a posh seaside enclave ninety miles northwest of Los Angeles that boasts a large collection of king-size estates. Abbe is anxious to hear this expert's opinion of the Sands' newest—and Abbe insists last—great remodeling project. But that's really a secondary desire. More than anything, the Sands want Joni to come up with a plan to finish the project with a fitting landscape that will look and feel like a paradise.

Joni focuses her eyes on the passing scenery as Abbe chauffeurs her through Montecito's elegant one-street downtown. They turn off onto a residential side street and ride up a short hill that flattens into a long mesa. As they climb onto the mesa, the houses grow from California ranch-style designs, looking deceptively small because of their single-story structure, to large, walled-in Spanish Colonial Revival mansions. The landscape evolves from compact lawns bordered by mature, well-tended shrubs, to story-high hedges hiding interiors of manicured green and full-grown gardens. The narrow road gets narrower and tall trees and tree-like bushes fill the view—lush but orderly, a neatnik's version of woodsiness.

Suddenly, shockingly, the Sands' house jumps into view from behind a street-side lineup of towering eucalyptus trees, their sensuous flesh-toned trunks looking like giants' legs. The old mansion is surrounded by nearly barren grounds. It is a giant diamond on a deserted mesa. It is a sight worthy of that all-purpose expression suited to occasions of speechlessness, and Joni manages to keep it to herself. "Wow!" she thinks.

Only months earlier, the Sands moved from a comfortable but modest home in the San Fernando Valley, a sprawling extension of Los Angeles, to Montecito, an opulent old community that borders Santa Barbara. It is a move comparable to leaving Brooklyn for Westchester County, but with a beach thrown in. They went from a tract house to what Joni describes simply as "a really spectacular setting" in a neighborhood of spectaculars. Now they are surrounded by some of the premier private gardens in the state. In a place like this, a garden borders on being a need, not just a want. As Abbe eases the Range Rover through the iron gate and up to the house, Joni feels excited. "This is great," she thinks. "This is going to be fun."

The Sands' seven-bedroom house sits like a slightly off-center centerpiece on a flat of land. It is nearly a hundred years old—almost ancient by the standards of the western half of the country, where the population was relatively sparse until after World War II. It is a squarish two-level with brown-hued shingles running down the side of its top story to meet a lighter golden-brown stucco-sided first story. It looks more Eastern than Western in design, perhaps reflecting the East Coast origins of its first owners. One local architecture book describes the house as an example of a subspecies of Craftsman Movement design called Bay Region Tradition, a style especially favored in San Francisco and inspired by Swiss chalets and the shingle-style mansions of the Eastern United States. Despite the house's large size, it has a homey quality that suggests grandmothers and good kitchen smells.

When the Sands first saw the house about a year earlier, it was a mess, its inside and outside neglected for years. Since then, they have acted as medical directors overseeing the reconstruction of a badly mutilated body. The house demanded more than a simple face-lift. Workers replaced a broken foundation. Painters repainted the outside and inside, every wall and every shingle. Roofers replaced the slate roof. Electricians rewired its large kitchen and installed fashionable, up-to-date appliances. Carpenters added new windows, doors, and custom cabinets. They sanded, polished, and resealed the old wooden floors. They stripped layers of paint from the banister of the main stairway, revealing rich brown mahogany.

The stale, musty odor that permeated every crevice of the house when the Sands bought it has vanished. The house is young again, as fresh as it was the day in 1906 when an artist from Nantucket moved his family across the country, becoming the first of a string of families that would live in this house. Now it hosts a new family—a mother, a father, a daughter, a son, and a big-hearted dog. Once again, the house is a home and the picture-perfect scene is complete—almost.

The yard remains a single, glaring problem. It is screaming for attention. At first glance, it looks nearly empty but for a couple of rows of eucalyptus trees suitable for feeding koalas (of which there are none), an uninvited pumpkin patch, a few shrubs, some small palms probably planted from seed by passing birds. But the longer you look, the more there is to see, all arranged in no clear pattern. A grand old coast live oak, native to this part of California, and a young olive tree, native to Spain, are the yard's most notable features. Some small orange trees appear here and there. A rosebush pops up in a far corner, a persimmon tree grows nearby. There is no grass, no ground cover. There is, instead, nearly an acre of bare dirt, an unrestrained sandbox whose grains have been mixed with clay and packed firm. Add rainwater and the yard becomes the key ingredient in a recipe for mud-caked shoes and dirty footprints tracked across a clean kitchen floor.

When Abbe and Dennis Sands first saw the yard, a nearly impenetrable tangle of trees and shrubs covered it. It resembled a jungle if jungles grew on the Southern California coast. A lot of people had passed up this property, even though it was priced lower than the large lots and stately homes typical in this neighborhood. To most potential buyers, its problems probably seemed overwhelming, the task of renovating too enormous. But Abbe and Dennis had already been through two renovations on smaller homes in Los Angeles. They knew how to envision a drab box as a small castle, and they knew how to organize a stream of workers to make the transformation happen.

"We knew that the house was a good house," Abbe says. "Architecturally, it had a lot of merit and we could see that and we just knew that." She pauses. "Actually, we didn't know. We just wondered if we were the people to take this project on." The doubts, the broken appliances, windows that wouldn't open, and a grime-caked kitchen didn't scare them away. And neither did the jungle. They figured that in time they could turn the yard into some version of paradise. But before that could happen, the jungle would have to be tamed.

The day the deal on the house was closed, the Sands had

a six-man crew on site to start paring away the plants, even before workers arrived to begin restoring the house itself. Abbe and Dennis slowly learned that their yard problem was larger than they anticipated. The stands of cypress that anchored the edges of the property, which had seemed so beautiful, proved to be largely dead, held together in rigor mortis by webs of old vines. The trees became falling timber in windstorms, a fire hazard during heat waves.

On and off for nearly six months, workers trimmed, cut, and carried away the dead cypress and other overgrown plants, then dug out stumps. They uncovered a few hidden gems: the old oak, the orange trees, a cement slab perfect for basketball that lay behind the house. Something that appeared to be a young, crooked monkey puzzle tree was tucked into a back corner.

Neighbors would stroll by and encourage the Sands. More than once, Dennis arrived at the house to find a few of the nosier neighbors taking self-guided tours of the project, inside and out. Occasionally, a fire truck would roll past and the crew would honk and wave. "They were just thrilled that this old house was being resurrected and cleared, because it was such a fire hazard to everyone in the area," Abbe recalls. "Everybody was very happy that it was cleaned up. Now they're so-o-o-o anxious to see it change again."

Montecito pushes into the foothills of the Santa Ynez Mountains. It is far enough from the biggest population centers of Southern California to feel remote, like a privileged island with calm beaches. Its founding residents included old-money families with Eastern ties. They were first drawn to the area as a vacation and summer escape during the late 1800s and early 1900s. Then, during the roaring twenties and later, Montecito became a year-round home. With the post-WWII rise of the movie industry in Los Angeles, it has become a distant suburb for wealthy entertainers and movie-industry executives. The houses here range in size from modest to immense, but most are larger than average.

The Sands live in one of Montecito's mid-range neighborhoods, an area that would be considered top-of-the-heap in most other communities of similar size. They and their neighbors know they live in a special place. And now the neighbors want reassurance that paradise—or at least landscape conformity—is still a possibility on the acre that stands out on their hedge-lined street as boldly as a landing strip in a rain forest. They want the open dirt expanse covered with something green and colorful.

"It's very interesting when you take on a project like this in a neighborhood. It's amazing how many people come out of the woodwork to lend an opinion or give you their card," Abbe says with a mix of amusement and exasperation. "There isn't a day that goes by that we don't get some landscaper or landscape architect putting a card in our mailbox. They see dollar signs. 'Wow, they need irrigation, they need this . . . ' Of course we know what we need. It just takes a while to get there. But it can't be fast enough for everybody."

Sometimes the pressure to do something soon comes from unexpected sources. As the Sands were planning their son's seventh birthday party, the boy asked his mother if she didn't feel embarrassed by the empty yard. "Yeah," Abbe told him, "I'm a little anxious for it to change."

Gardening, as virtually any gardening magazine will tell you, has become America's number-one leisure activity. This assertion is supported by polls commissioned by the National Gardening Association, a nonprofit organization best known for its magazine, *National Gardening*. The NGA polls have found that about three-quarters of America's households participate in some kind of gardening activity, either indoors or outdoors. That means around 72 million households are each spending an average of more than $340 a year to plant or maintain everything from potted bromeliads that decorate a coffee table to weed-infested lawns that fill a back yard.

What the polls don't measure, and what the magazines don't talk about, is avidness. Not all those gardeners out there are gardening because they love to garden. Many are reluctant gardeners. They garden because they have to, not because they want to. They garden because they have been thrown into the role of caretaker for a piece of land simply because shelter happens to come attached to the land. Whether it be a condominium patio plot or a ranch-size lot, that land wants. It wants plants. It wants sidewalks. It wants patios. It wants water, and more than just about anything, it wants time and effort. Indeed, a piece of land can be about as pleasant and demanding as a two-year-old child mid-tantrum.

Just as the land wants, the landowner wants. Most landowners, including reluctant gardeners, want that land to have what it whines for most: an attractive landscape. The problem is figuring out how to get it. Is it better, the reluctant gardener may wonder, to transform yourself into an avid gardener, to throw yourself whole-hog into the landscape effort and design and plant your own yard, create a lush retreat and gardening showcase? Or is it better to hang on to your reluctant-gardener sensibilities and create a conforming landscape without investing too much time or effort, simply to plant that imperfect lawn, a border of daylilies, a tall shade tree, a few pansies and impatiens for bold spring color, and then do the minimal amount to keep it growing? Judging from the look of most American yards and landscapes, we are a nation of reluctant gardeners.

We are also a nation of innovators, and one of our greatest, most popular innovations is hiring an expert. As our baby boomers settle comfortably into middle age, the tendency to hire experts gets even stronger, particularly when it comes to home improvement. Another survey, this one commissioned by a consortium of nursery and landscape industry organizations, found that in a recent year 17.6 million American households spent $13.4 billion on professional lawn and landscape services. Half of that amount was spent to hire people to do the routine mowing and hedging. Also, nearly half of that amount was spent by people between the ages of thirty and forty-nine.

The trend toward hiring experts has made the design segment the fastest growing of the landscape services industry. In a single recent year, American households spent $869 million in professional landscape design services, more than double the amount spent the year before. That doesn't include the costs of actually building and installing the designed landscapes. These design services were performed by everyone from formally trained, licensed landscape architects to self-trained garden designers.

Three months after workers finished renovating the Sands' house and cleaning up the overgrown yard, Dennis and Abbe fell into the statistical trend. They followed through on what is certainly every reluctant gardener's personal fantasy. They didn't roll up their sleeves and spend backbreaking Saturdays planning a landscape, turning soil, selecting and planting greenery, babying sod. They called in an expert.

Joni met the Sands for the first time several years earlier when they lived in the same neighborhood as her stepsister, Suzanne. Suzanne introduced them after the Sands admired a planting plan the young landscape architect created for Suzanne's own yard. The Sands liked it because it used plants they had never seen in their neighborhood, plants that seemed designed to tolerate the hot, dry San Fernando Valley summers. They liked the plan because it looked different. And once they met her, they liked the plan's designer.

The Sands and Joni all grew up in the seamless collection of small towns and big cities that make up the Los Angeles metropolitan area. Dennis, in his late forties, is a musician who parlayed his talent into a career as a music scoring mixer, orchestrating and recording film scores. If you've seen *Forrest Gump* or *An American President* or *The First Wives' Club*, you've heard some of the soundtracks Dennis has helped create. Cautious and reserved with strangers, warm and friendly with friends and family, he projects the image of a man who works hard, is devoted to his family, appreciates baseball, and, in the right setting, can pound a mean beat on a drum set. He relishes a life that allows him to spend at least part of his time working from a home office, in a comfortable uniform of jeans and T-shirt.

Abbe, talkative and ready with funny one-liners, spent twenty years in the television and film industry before quitting to raise their kids. She is the daughter of a homemaker and a policeman who liked to do projects around their house. Sometimes it would be building a fence. Other times it would be making a garden of unusual plants, to which Abbe, a kid entranced with the beach and its social scene, barely paid attention.

Joni grew up mostly in the L.A. suburbs closest to the ocean, but what she cherishes the most are the summers before her adolescence that she spent hundreds of miles away from the city. During those summers, her mother would load Joni and her two older brothers into the family car and drive north to the Sierra Nevada forests around Lake Tahoe. There, the foursome would set up housekeeping in a campground. Joni's business-executive father would join them when he could break away from his work. Those summer camping trips were the incubator for her acute affinity for nature. She loved being in the outdoors, away from cars, and among the trees. Now thirty-two, Joni finds herself engaged in a career that at least occasionally allows her to pay homage to the wildland landscapes she first explored on those childhood trips.

Joni climbs out of Abbe's Range Rover and walks to the front of the house. In a way, it feels familiar. Joni, after all, designed a landscape for the Sands once before. But this is a very different world. Abbe warned her in earlier phone conversations that the new yard is bigger and more open than the old one. But Joni hadn't imagined it would be this big or this exposed. In a neighborhood where privacy is guarded by high walls, high hedges, and high fences, this yard stands out like neon on a dark night.

Joni silently regrets that she hadn't seen the property earlier. Maybe she could have saved more of the remnants of the old landscape. "I probably should have been down there before they did a lot of the clearing," she says later. The nearly plant-free lot shows little evidence of what sort of garden might have been there before. She will have to start from scratch, like an artist facing an empty canvas. Only this canvas is surrounded by dozens of beautiful landscapes, the sort that are the subject of photo spreads in slick magazines about fancy homes and fancy gardens. Other landscape architects, like anxious artists with their paintbrushes at the ready, are waiting in the shadows, wanting to get their hands on the property. Working here might be like painting an empty canvas in the middle of New York's Metropolitan Museum of Art on a free-entrance day for critics. It has challenge and visibility. Whether she does good work or bad, it will be noticed.

Joni admires the large oak and then follows Abbe up a couple of steps, across a broken red-brick patio, and through the perfectly finished front door into the Sands' new home. Dennis leaves his upstairs office and meets the women in the entrance hall. Rich wood floors, banisters, and stairs delight the senses of sight and smell and touch in the way a single chocolate truffle delights the sense of taste, smoothly and deliciously. Before they confront the yard, they tour what is now a dream house. Joni follows the Sands from room to room, most sparely or barely furnished. She follows them to the downstairs sunroom, aptly named for the three walls of sunlight-filled windows. It was probably once the studio of the home's first owner, artist William Starbuck Macy. They lead her upstairs, where workers converted one of the seven bedrooms into a grand bathroom. All the while, Joni glances out windows to take in the views of the yard, trying to imprint in her mind what the family sees from each room.

Finally, Abbe and Joni return downstairs and sit at the dining-room table, where Abbe has laid out a collection of home-and-garden books. The pages are turned to photographs of favorite landscapes. The work begins.

Joni Janecki is the lead character in a small, young firm that bears her name. She has a sense of humor and a pleasant manner that clients like. As one client says, she is easy to talk to and natural. She freely flashes a smile of perfect white teeth, wears her brown hair long and straight, and favors jeans, loose-fitting slacks, full blouses, comfortable shoes. Down-to-earth and common-sensical, she appreciates the part of being a landscape architect that often—though not always—frees her from the discomforts of corporate attire that is heavy on form and light on function.

Her firm handles a wide range of landscape projects. In a single week, she may begin a landscape design on a major corporate headquarters, consult with a homeowner, bid on a chance to restore a park's creek bed, consider developing an institution's landscape master plan, work on a restoration plan for a section of grassland, and review construction of an urban pedestrian alley. One underlying theme ties all her work together. She loves native plants—the grasses, shrubs, trees, and flowers which preceded European settlement in America and which grace the country's shrinking wildlands. She advocates using native plants as much as possible and promotes natural-looking grounds. The résumé she keeps on hand for clients says her firm's "philosophy is to bring the site conditions, program, client and user needs together with the natural environment."

That philosophy was epitomized at the Sands' old house in the San Fernando Valley. Someone else might have looked at it and seen a cheek-by-jowl tract of look-alike homes sprawling for miles in either direction. Joni saw the dry river bed that was there before the construction crew arrived. Someone else might have checked the regional gardening guide and selected whatever the nursery had available to plant, from daylilies to geraniums. Joni investigated what plants thrived in the area before the first bulldozer arrived and which might thrive again. Then she tracked down a nursery that carried those plants. As other landscape architects would have, she considered microclimates and macroclimates, soil types and site grades, and simple aesthetics. As only some other landscape architects might have, she considered ecology and biology.

Garden centers, wholesale growers, seed companies, garden writers, gardeners, landscape designers, and landscape architects constitute a giant gardening culture in America. That culture shapes what we see in the human-made landscape virtually everywhere we go, every day. Like any culture, the gardening culture is imbued with its own unspoken rules. Among the most common, most powerful, are these: new and different is usually good; the best plant is one that will grow under almost universal conditions; there is no such thing as too much lawn; and the bigger and brighter the flower, the better. Driven by these guidelines, America's gardening culture has managed to fill the country with created landscapes that typically have very little relationship to the local wildlands. It can be difficult now to distinguish one region of America from another, based solely on plants used in created landscapes. The human-made landscape has become as removed from the natural landscape as a fast-food hamburger patty is from the cow. As at least one landscape architect has suggested, America's created landscape, the landscape we see every day, has become McDonaldized.

Joni is part of the gardening culture simply by being a landscape architect. But she is also something of a rebel. By using native plants and local materials, she is breaking away from the culture's dominant forces. She is part of a larger movement that is gradually shaking up the mainstream, slowly pushing America's created landscape to replicate more closely the local natural landscape by including native plants and designing with the look of the wild landscape in mind. Those wild landscapes are not just the sum of so many plants and other natural elements. They are the product of hundreds of complex relationships and processes in nature and have not been significantly altered by human intervention. Sometimes they look ordered, sometimes chaotic. Always, they define a place. Underlying this native-plant movement is the often unspoken hope that if people have more daily contact and experience with native plants, they will come to appreciate the plants' wildland homes more, and the nature at work there.

A growing number of landscape architects are, like Joni, trying to bridge the gulf between the landscapes we see every day around our homes and workplaces and in our towns and the wild landscapes that we know less about and may even fear. They are trying to make nature familiar. Their work is consistent with the early history of landscape architecture in this country.

The profession's first leaders pioneered natural-looking created landscapes. They used native plants and designed with sensitivity to a region's natural history, imitating local scenery. Often those created scenes idealized nature, heightening certain beloved images—the gentle rolling meadow, the grove of wide-brimmed trees, the rocky nook. But even in their idealized state, these created landscapes came closer to the reality of local nature, including its complexity and subtlety, than the standard landscape of today, where evidence of human control and mastery over plant behavior is boldly celebrated.

The late-twentieth-century revival of this earlier design approach retools the gardening culture's dominant definition of nature as anything green that grows. Nature, instead, refers to the natural elements—the plants and animals—that existed before European settlement in North America prompted headlong change and destruction of so much of the continent's wildlands. It also refers to the processes that organize those elements in the wildlands into habitats and communities. The revival recognizes that any act of landscaping or gardening involves human manipulation of plants and environments. But unlike mainstream gardening and design, it incorporates ecological sensitivity. It challenges the gardening industry's axiom to use "the right plant for the right place." It suggests that the definition of the right plant goes beyond basic cultivation issues like watering regimens and sunlight requirements. The right plant is one that supports birds, insects, and other creatures, doesn't require pounds of pesticides to maintain, has adapted over eons to the local climate and rainfall, and defines a place by reflecting the local wildlands—the places where plants have been left mostly untouched by people.

Sweeping changes are more the stuff of fiction than history. Any change comes in small increments, small steps, often taken by ordinary people working in quiet ways. Usually it is only after a series of small steps that change is noticed. And then it can seem almost a revolution to those who weren't paying attention. Joni Janecki takes her small steps to change gardening culture in her daily work, designing landscapes for clients who give her leeway to follow her instincts, even as she helps them discover their own vision of paradise.

The notion of an earthly paradise was introduced to the Western world by the Greek soldier and writer Xenophon. His military expeditions during the third and fourth centuries B.C. took him to Persia, where he admired the lush enclosed garden estates of kings and nobles. The gardens, home to birds and wild mammals, served both as beautiful reserves and as hunting grounds. Xenophon called them *paradeisos.*

Today, paradise still connotes a beautiful place, particularly a beautiful landscape. Most versions encourage tranquillity, are visually attractive, and include natural elements—plants, water, stone, and even animals—although not necessarily as they are found in the wild. A paradise also feels personal, even if its views are expansive. A person enjoying paradise feels part of the landscape, not apart from it. Yet even when it includes all these characteristics, one man's paradise can be another's anti-paradise. A desert paradise to one person may be a desert wasteland to another. Whether a place looks and feels like paradise depends on the beholder.

For a landscape architect, the beholders are the clients, and the first step in any project is meeting with the clients to find out what they do and don't like, what they do and don't want—how clients see paradise. To make the most of her single day in Montecito, Joni asked the Sands to start thinking about what they like and want before she flew down.

Abbe took to the assignment as naturally as fragrance to a flower. When Abbe used to produce television commercials and wanted to get a certain look for a set, she did her research by collecting visual images from magazines, books, and real life. "I would rip pictures out and sort of go location scouting and take snapshots of other people's houses so I would be able to say, 'Okay, this is what I like and this the feel I would like to accomplish.' "

Now she sits with Joni at the dining-room table, pointing

out the landscapes she and Dennis both like among the photos she has found in the stack of books and magazines. Neither of the Sands knows much about plants, but they know what they like in overall effect. Joni occasionally takes notes as she examines the photos. Among Abbe's favorites is one that shows a large house with an entrance flanked by a gorgeous perennial garden. Lavenders, grays, and reds fill the beds and the whole effect is of a Mediterranean garden, what you might find at an Italian villa or country home. It is well planned but informal and cheerful. It is the photo that will stick in Joni's mind the most as she later begins designing the Sands' landscape.

The Sands have spent several months in the neighborhood and have explored it by car and on foot. They have spotted other yards with features they like and now, as Dennis joins the two women and Abbe closes the landscape books, the Sands offer to take the landscape architect on a tour to point out some of their favorites. They climb into the Land Rover and Abbe drives, while Dennis navigates. They become mobile looky-loos, stopping at the ends of driveways and peering through gates to examine walls, pathways, and plants.

This drive is oddly nostalgic for Joni. As a teenager, after her parents divorced, she and her mother moved to nearby Santa Barbara. For entertainment, Joni would occasionally roam Montecito's streets with friends and sneak over the walls of some of the larger estates just to admire the gardens. Driving those same streets again, sneaking looks at gardens, feels like déjà vu, but now the drivers are *clients* and she is preparing to design one of those gardens.

When they finally return to the Sands' house, the three

share a lunch of deli sandwiches at the big round table near the fireplace in the spacious kitchen. This is a cook's dream kitchen. Handcrafted cabinets surround an industrial-strength stove and refrigerator. Abbe later jokes that she rarely cooks but does great take-out. As Joni eats, she makes note of the view from the kitchen windows that flank the room. One line of windows looks out to a sunny space in the back yard, which is bordered on one side by a fence and on the other by the house. That spot might be perfect for a swimming pool. The other windows look out to the street. This house was once alone on the mesa. Over the years, as land was divided and the mesa became a neighborhood, a street was laid that ran along the side of the house rather than its true front. So now kitchen windows and a door to the kitchen stare directly at the street, while the house's front is perpendicular to the street and overlooks the largest uninterrupted section of the nearly nude yard. Joni realizes that one of her design challenges will be to configure a landscape that makes the front door a focal point again and downplays the side-door kitchen entrance.

Through the day, the designer walks the yard. She takes photos from every angle, intending to reconstruct views once she is back in her office. She keeps asking the Sands questions to flesh out their dream. Would they like some kind of water feature? Do they have guests often and need a garden designed for entertaining? Do they want an herb garden? A vegetable garden? Do they want a play area for the kids?

The front fence and gates need to be replaced, Abbe and Dennis say. They want a definite entry into the front of the house. They want some kind of designated space for their dog, a bear-size charmer who includes the mail carrier among his best pals. They want a pool house and a pool, but they don't want the yard to feel formal. They want to preserve views of the gray-green hills rising to the north, backdrop for the south-facing seaside community. They know from living through a recent drought of several years' duration that they want plants that don't require lots of water. Otherwise, they have no specific plant requirements, save one: Dennis wants a monkey puzzle tree that is big and clearly visible.

Just before 6:00 p.m., after nearly eight hours with the Sands, Joni collects her canvas satchel and camera and Dennis races to get her back to the airport in time for her flight home. She is the last to board the plane, and as she settles into her seat, the enormity of the project she has taken on begins to sink in. The Sands' demands are relatively few; she will have a lot of creative freedom. She will be able to follow her devotion to native plants to a degree she never has been able to on a private residence. She will be doing all this from her small, three-person firm. Anything she designs will likely be seen and considered by other landscape architects working in the area, which includes veterans whose work she has admired for years. This project could give Joni L. Janecki & Associates a toehold in one of the most notable landscaped communities in California.

By the time the plane lands, the firm's principal landscape architect feels perfectly overwhelmed.

II

LANDSCAPE ARCHITECTS ARE NOT THE ONLY people who design the spaces between buildings—from back yards to public parks and corporate campuses. Under the heading "landscape" in a typical phone book's yellow pages, there are dozens of listings for landscape contractors and landscapers and a few for people who identify themselves as garden designers. The listings far outnumber those under the heading "landscape architect." Some of those landscape contractors and landscapers are also licensed landscape architects, but most are not. They may have backgrounds and training in construction or horticulture or both, but they haven't gone through the same academic training and licensing that most landscape architects must complete, which give landscape architects a foot up when bidding on large-scale projects.

As professions go, that of licensed landscape architect represents a fairly small club. There are only about 25,000 in the United States, small potatoes compared to, say, lawyers (about 816,000) and physicians (about 460,000). They are even outnumbered by architects who design buildings (about 85,000). More people can say they have visited a doctor or lawyer than can say they have been in a landscape architect's office. Yet every day millions of people see the results of the landscape architect's labors, often without recognition. Their work is on constant view, usually public view, and often in the most prominent places.

Landscape architects are the elite of the rock, dirt, and plant world workers. They can point to the likes of Frederick Law Olmsted, one of the founders of the profession and co-designer of many must-see places in America, including New York's Central Park, as their professional ancestors. One conservative estimate attributes to landscape architects the planning and design of fewer than five percent of America's human-made landscapes. Yet the profession's impact reaches beyond the boundaries of its own designs because the landscape architect's work sets the standard. Homeowners, amateur gardeners, and landscape professionals of various sorts often copy the work of well-known landscape architects, past and present. Garden and home-improvement magazines tout work by landscape architects in glossy to-drool-over photos that make the average home gardener wilt from envy.

Despite the impact of their work, what landscape architects do has remained mostly a mystery to the general public. As one young practitioner complained, landscape architecture can be a conversation stopper. When people hear he is a landscape architect, either they stumble for a response while silently trying to recall what that is or they quickly ask how much he charges for lawn maintenance.

Landscape architects don't mow lawns. Rarely do they put their hands to soil or plug a plant into the ground. But they can envision and then draft plans and draw colorful renderings of what a landscape might become, including not just the planted areas but also the courtyards, pathways, and other features. They can analyze the way the land rises and falls, curves and straightens, and take those features into account as they design. When money and motivation come together, landscape architects help make those imagined landscapes a reality. They know which type of brick or stone would create the best effect, and the best among them can identify which plants are perfectly suited for which place. They follow their plans and renderings with even more detailed documents directing where to plant the trees, where to install a watering system, where to build a wall, where to place a bench or a fountain, how much dirt to dig and move and shape and form. Landscape architects can do the work that people who like a nice landscape, but not gardening, feel totally unprepared to do themselves.

Landscape architects tend to specialize. Sometimes people think "garden designer" when they hear "landscape architect." Landscape architects, though, are quick to point out that garden design is only one kind of work included within their profession, and not all landscape architects practice it. Some are more interested in urban design, arranging and enhancing the sidewalks, alleys, and resting places of city streets. Some plan whole communities, focusing on traffic patterns and housing density and how they affect a place's livability and its relation to natural features. Some who practice garden design focus less on home garden design and more on designing public green spaces such as parks. And some focus on restoring natural habitats, returning the wildness to areas that humans have disturbed or destroyed. Where there is disordered land, landscape architects are there to put things in place, either as they once were or in a new form.

Their profession "applies artistic and scientific principles to the research, planning, design and management of both natural and built environments," according to the definition adopted by the American Society of Landscape Architects. They do their work "with a concern for the stewardship and conservation of natural, constructed and human resources." If they do their work right, the "resulting environments shall serve useful, aesthetic, safe and enjoyable purposes." This sounds like a whole lot more than planning and planting an attractive garden. It reflects a training and professional history that, on landscape architecture's best days, emphasizes a sensitivity to ecology that is typically glossed over or ignored by other garden design and landscape occupations. And as they do their work, the best landscape architects try to create a paradise by design.

Joni works in a recycled building that falls short of paradise but is heavy on charm. Her offices occupy what used to be the dining hall of an old sash mill, the place where workers who milled windows and doors and doorways stopped midday to refuel. The mill closed long ago and its buildings have been remodeled into low-rise offices for an eclectic mix that includes engineers, hairstylists, cookie makers, and candy sellers.

The old dining hall is divided into three rooms. There is a large one where most of the small firm's work gets done, a medium one that serves as Joni's office, and a tiny one about the size of a walk-in closet for the photocopy machine and office supplies. On this late-fall morning, Joni sits on a tall stool at a high old table in the middle of the main room. The ceiling is pitched and rough wood beams are exposed. The floor is a honey-colored wood. Native-plant posters hang on the walls. Colored plans from other projects, a combination of realistic and abstract art, are tacked up among the posters. Bunches of dried flowers hang here and there; a dried tree branch decorates one narrow strip of white wall. Desks and worktables, a coat tree, and two computers are arranged along the peripheries of the room. Outside, it is cold and rainy; here, the heater has barely started the job of warming the office. Nevertheless, it feels cozy.

Robin MacLean, one of the firm's three landscape architects, sits at a corner table and reviews a plant list for a new park the firm is helping to design. She is racing a deadline to get the groups of plants color-coded on a large map of the park. Joni has pitched in to help for a few minutes before she begins her own work. She uses colored pencils to shade designated planting sections on the map. As she colors, the map begins to look like a flowing mosaic of interlocking shapes.

Jazz plays softly over office speakers connected to the CD player hidden in the tiny office-supplies room. After a moment Robin considers a decision made days ago that changed a planting scheme for a hard-to-reach strip in the park. "It seems like taking the grassland out of the buffer is a good idea," she says.

"Think so?" Joni responds.

"Yeah."

"I just don't know how they'd mow it or take care of it," Joni agrees.

They keep coloring. It is tedious but satisfying, and one of the easiest parts of the job. It doesn't require negotiating, it doesn't require educating, it doesn't require considering the ecological impact or the maintenance consequences of a decision. It doesn't require pulling a creative design from thin air. It doesn't require practicing a form of mind-reading to make sure they understand what a client wants. In short, it doesn't require most of the skills a landscape architect has to employ to varying degrees with every project. It just requires an ability to color within the lines.

Drawing those lines was one of the first things that attracted Joni to the profession. She took some architectural drafting classes in high school and thought that she might want to be an architect. Then she enrolled in Santa Barbara City College and took botany classes from a teacher named Al Flinck.

Broad-shouldered and husky, Flinck fills a classroom with contagious enthusiasm for plants and their role in the natural world. His expressive blue eyes work like exclamation points during his lectures, widening and narrowing as information pours forth. Under Flinck's tutelage, Joni found direction. She fell in love with botany, expecially the field classes in which Flinck sent his students into the foothills and canyons that encircle Santa Barbara to study the native flora. Not incidentally, she also fell in love with a fellow student, Andrew Janecki.

Flinck suggested Joni put her interest in plants together with her interest in design and apply to the landscape-architecture program at California Polytechnic State University at San Luis Obispo, a town in cattle-ranching country about an hour's drive north of Santa Barbara. She took Flinck's advice and was soon spending long hours in studio classes at Cal Poly.

Like most landscape-architecture students, Joni started with graphics and basic design classes. Then she progressed to more complicated design classes, including some devoted entirely to the tedious task of creating construction drawings, and others devoted to analyzing the defining features of a parcel of land, its slopes and dips. She took classes on irrigation-system design, and on regional landscape assessment. By her last year, she was working on real design proposals with real deadlines in the maze of cubicles that forms a cavernous studio classroom for Cal Poly's landscape-architecture students. There, students work around the clock as their final semester approaches its end, designing, drawing, coloring, collaborating, and sharing late-night pizzas.

The benefit of all this hard work is a transcript with good grades, and Joni earned that. But the grand prize is a job with the kind of firm that can make for a dazzling résumé while a young landscape architect fulfills the apprenticeship required before taking licensing exams.

Joni began her job search with some uncertainty. "I don't know if I really knew what I wanted to do. I definitely had an affinity for natural stuff and not the contrived landscapes," she recalls. "And I was very particular about where I went to work. I wanted to work for somebody who did more than just put trees in the ground."

She turned to her professors for advice and one suggested she try interviewing with Emmet L. Wemple, a veteran Southern California landscape architect. Wemple was internationally known and had created landscapes for many of Southern California's best-known public places, including the J. Paul Getty Museum in Malibu. He was generally considered one of the deans of landscape architecture in Southern California and was noted for his interest in native plants and the region's natural landscape. On paper at least, Wemple and his firm seemed a perfect fit for Joni, and Wemple apparently agreed. He gave her her first job. Soon she was driving hundreds of miles a week on the Los Angeles freeways, visiting the clients and sites she was working on for Wemple's firm.

It was great training. "That's why I have this office today," Joni says matter-of-factly. Because she worked for Wemple, she says, clients assume (or at least hope) she brings the same high standards to a project.

Joni admired Wemple and appreciated the solid training she was getting at his firm. But the work coming out of the office wasn't the kind she wanted to do. The elder architect's personal interest in native plants and natural landscapes seemed to get lost in the firm's commissions for large-scale landscapes emphasizing exotic plantings and huge fountains fabricated from imported stone. The mass and scale and ostentation contradicted Joni's own emerging views of design. Sometimes they conflicted with her personal values.

"We did one project with Chinese slate and we had giant entablatures, which were like eight inches thick and three feet deep, for a fountain," she recalls. She found herself crying on the way to that job as she considered the political situation and the labor conditions where that stone came from. "I just knew what was going on in China to bring that here. I didn't think it was right and it made me feel bad."

After three and a half years at Wemple's firm, Joni had her license and decided she needed more money. By then, she had married Drew, who was in law school, and she had become the main household support. Also, she wanted to do work that came closer to her growing interest in natural-looking landscapes that recall the scenery found in local wildlands. So she left Wemple and went to work for another former Wemple employee who had started his own firm. The pay was better, but the work still didn't play to Joni's landscape interests. There were a lot of malls and a lot of office buildings with fairly conventional landscapes. There was also the increasingly exhausting L.A. traffic. It was all made tolerable by the knowledge that Drew would be finishing law school and she could rethink her career path. When he graduated, Drew found a job as a public defender in Santa Cruz and the couple moved north.

Santa Cruz is a seven-hour drive from Los Angeles. Sometimes it seems light-years away. With a population of about 50,000, it is an ink spot on the map compared to L.A.'s sprawling bulk. It has a University of California campus on one hilly inland edge, bordered by open space and a redwood forest. At the far seaside end opening onto Monterey Bay, Santa Cruz sports a dense collection of motels representing just about every bargain chain in the country and a Coney

Island-style boardwalk with a giant roller coaster and ferris wheels. In between is the town center with its eclectic mix of shops and restaurants whose offerings, if pulled into a single cafeteria, would make just about everyone at the United Nations feel at home. Mountain bicyclists with muddy tires, white kids with dreadlocks, women who wore Doc Martens before they became fashion statements, men who show feelings, surfers who live for nothing else, computer entrepreneurs, college teachers, and a guy in a clown suit who puts money in expired parking meters share the streets with tourists. Santa Cruz is a definite place, a quirky island within a space-rich region within a crowded state of mind, and everyone here knows it.

"I felt pretty depleted after I left L.A.," Joni says. So she spent her first months in Santa Cruz simply enjoying living in a smaller community that revels in community. Situated on the edge of a bay on the edge of a continent and on the edge of a mountain range beyond the edge of the Silicon Valley and the San Francisco Bay, Santa Cruz fit one of Joni's basic requirements for habitability: "I'm really into edges and being on the edge."

While she considered what to do next, she rode her bicycle, worked out, and explored the area. She knew she didn't want to work for somebody else again. She didn't want to "go through these emotional things" about land use and whether what she was doing was right or wrong, and then end up having to do what she believed was wrong or lose her job. She called her mentor Wemple for advice. He encouraged her to send her résumé to the main architect at U.C. Santa Cruz. She did and the school invited her to join the list of landscape architects who bid to do campus projects. It was a good start, and from a drafting table in her apartment living room, she began Joni L. Janecki & Associates.

It has been three years since Joni started her firm and in that time she has hired two other landscape architects, a part-time bookkeeper, and each summer, a student intern. She has moved her office twice to accommodate its growth. She says she rarely makes plans beyond the next six months. But now, as she sits absorbed in coloring the park planting plan, she knows that a recent flurry of new work she has lured into the office means the next year could be pivotal. It will challenge her ability to organize and oversee several significant projects simultaneously. It will prove whether she can expand her business while maintaining an office atmosphere that keeps creative people productive and happy. It will test her will to create landscapes which are consistent with her passion for natural-looking scenery and native plants and which remain true to her ideals about environmental sensitivity and sustainability.

Joni's ideals call for landscapes dominated by plants that are comfortable in the local climate, so they require little or no supplemental watering or fertilizing. Usually, in Joni's mind, this means using plants that are native to the region, that help define a place as distinctive, that link it to what grew there before the bulldozers arrived. But it can include exotics that provide some special characteristic, such as fruit for eating or nectar, or that are able to grow in urban spots where no native can. Joni's ideals call for landscapes that provide a habitat for the birds and other native creatures whose homes have been squeezed out by development. The best designs, she believes, also help people experience nature in at least a small way every day, and they don't add new problems to the environment. They may actually solve problems, often by returning a piece of the wildlands to damaged land, restoring a bit of the local ecology. Finally, Joni's ideals call for the created landscape to look good, to be the kind of place where people want to be, to be filled with the beauty, surprise, and mystery that make any created landscape work, no matter the type of plants.

After a few more minutes helping Robin, Joni decides she can't put off her own work any longer. She excuses herself and strides to her office, which is separated from the main room by a wall made of windowpanes and a door that is rarely closed. In her office, a bicycle leans against a bookcase. Her desk and work area take up one corner of the room. A glass-topped table that doubles as a conference table during staff meetings stands on one side of the room near windows that look out onto a small courtyard and neighboring offices.

A base map lies flat on the conference table. It is a blueprint that shows property lines, an outline of a house's footprint, and circles that indicate existing trees. Block hand printing on one corner identifies it as the base map for the Sands' residence.

It has been more than two months since Joni visited the Montecito property. In that time, between other projects, she has organized her notes and measurements of the Sands' lot. When the Sands were remodeling their house, they had an engineer draw a basic blueprint of the house's footprint. Joni combined that basic blueprint with the measurements she collected, and passed the information on to Robin, whose skills include literacy in computer-assisted design. Robin loaded the information into a computer program and created the base map.

Joni or Robin could have drawn the base map by hand, maybe in less time than it took to load information into the computer and manipulate the computer cursor. But having the base map in the computer saves time in the long run; it allows changes to be made more easily. The landscape architects won't have to draw a whole new base map by hand each time they make a change. Also, Joni notes, "Dennis is sort of into computers." She figures he will appreciate the effort and the effect.

Once Robin finished the base map, Joni mailed it to the Sands to review. Now it is back and, as Joni notes about the real property it represents, it is "desperately seeking landscape."

On the table next to the waiting base map, Joni has stacked a collection of books that Michael Bliss, a recent landscape-architecture graduate and her newest employee, fetched from the library. The books are about New England architecture and early houses of the region. Over the last few days, Joni has periodically flipped through the books, searching for inspiration for the house in Montecito. Leaning against the table is a three-foot by five-foot piece of foam-core board. Michael has pasted snapshots of the Sands' place onto the board in an arrangement that helps Joni recall the existing landscape.

For writers, it's the blank page. For actors, it's the empty stage. Everyone has to start with nothing at some point. For Joni, it's this base map, as big as a movie poster and decorated with a few stark lines representing boundaries, trees, and the house footprint. It is hard to face it before anything has been drawn on it. Somehow, just by sitting there in its near-nude state, it manages to call forth waves of insecurity about ability, creativity, and imagination.

When she finally sits down at the table, she stares anxiously at the base map. Then she gets up and saunters out to the main room and collects a box of colored pencils. She comes back into her office and finds a fine-point ink pen on her desk. She returns to the main room and tracks down an eraser. She comes back to the table and the waiting base map. She returns to the main room and looks for a straight edge and a template for circles. Finally, she is back in her office with everything she needs. She faces the base map again. With no more tasks to distract her, she has to begin drawing.

"I think what I'm going to suggest to them is that they have some formal—well, I don't want to say formal—some progression from the house up to the garden, so that it doesn't just become wild right at the door," she muses as she stares alternately at the base map and the photo board. "The house is so vertical, it's just sitting out on this island of dirt. It seems to need to step down and take up some more space before it turns wild."

She pulls a piece of onionskin tracing paper—she calls it

trace—off a thick roll and lays it across the base map. She uses a dark pencil to sketch variations of entry steps. Her strokes look effortless, quick, and efficient as they create a recognizable form. "Maybe this should be a big balustrade coming down like this." She sketches a balustrade. "Or maybe it should be some abstract thing with plants coming around it." She pushes the trace to move the balustrade away and now sketches an alternative, then abandons the trace altogether.

While this is the first time she has actually sat down to design on the base map since she met with the Sands, it isn't the first time she has drawn designs for the yard. She has a stack of trace paper with sketches of details that have come to her in spare moments and at unexpected times. She sketched a front gate with an upside-down arch at the top, an idea Abbe mentioned and Joni executed shortly after her Montecito visit. She sketched a pot-like fountain for a private niche in the garden one evening at home when the idea came to her as she was watching television with Drew. She has been thinking about the plan so much that now, as she prepares to draw the first hard draft, she has many of the basics worked out in her mind. The details will come over the next few hours. That is what the trace is for: working out the details.

Consider the plight of the bone-weary reluctant gardener. It is a warm spring Saturday, a glorious day free from office demands. The reluctant gardener believes it would be beyond delicious to spend the day on a chaise lounge beneath a shade tree, sipping lemonade, reading a book. It would be heaven.

However, the reluctant gardener's front yard has slipped below the neighborhood's admittedly modest standard for beauty and maintenance. The weeds that have transformed the back yard into an unfortunate example of neglect have worked their way into the front yard. They have overtaken everything, and now the reluctant gardener, growing more reluctant by the minute, realizes that an entire front-yard makeover is overdue. Are there simple steps the RG can take to eliminate the landscape embarrassment and fast?

Consider a few things C. Colston Burrell has learned from years of contemplating the typical home landscape. Burrell is a landscape architect in Minneapolis. Previously, he was curator of the native-plant garden at the National Arboretum in Washington, D.C. Botany, horticulture, and ecology are the tripod that supports his interest in native plants and in how to incorporate them into the human-made landscape. Drawing on research by University of Minnesota landscape architecture professor Joan Nassauer, Burrell has spent time trying to identify the notions that lead people to create the kinds of home landscapes which dominate the suburban and urban scene. This search has a purpose. Burrell figures that if he identifies and understands these notions, there might be a way to use them to bend people to create landscapes that are more nature-friendly, more attractive and usable by birds and animals, including people.

The everyday landscape, the way we organize plants in our own front yard, what landscape architects call the vernacular landscape (not to be confused with the intentional landscape, which is what they design), is the landscape that concerns Burrell most. Like it or not, he says, there is a typical suburban lot design we all naturally fall into when we create our yards. "It has very important elements, most of all the turf and the idea of tidiness," he told an audience at a Brooklyn Botanic Garden native-plant gardening symposium.

The tidiness and turf ideas got their start with Andrew Jackson Downing, an early-nineteenth-century plantsman and garden designer who is often credited with originating the idea of the suburb in America. Downing suggested that a man's devotion to his home, his attention to its neat appearance, both reflected and led to good citizenship and patriotism. (One wonders, if Downing had lived during the McCarthy era, would red-baiting have been less popular than snail-baiting? Would Hollywood stars have been blacklisted on the basis of the tidiness of their landscape rather than their politics?)

This link between good citizenship and front-yard tidiness has been perpetuated by others, including landscape architects, through the generations. As a result, "the average person is going to toe the neighborhood line and have turf from border to border, shrubs plastered against the house, scalped within an inch of their life," Burrell says. The shrubs against the house are commonly referred to as foundation plants, and "even though the house is securely grounded on its own, it must be further grounded with a mass of shrubs in front of it." In addition, the whole landscape will be "encased in landscape rock and fabric." These all add up to symbols of care. Typically, the vernacular landscape will include a tree at the corner of the yard or on the edge of the property.

There will be a clear view to the front door and a number of flower beds or islands. "Flowers are also a very important symbol of care because to tend a garden by nature implies that you are working with the landscape and showing good stewardship," Burrell notes.

In the vernacular landscape, anything related to natural balance, ecology, basic biology goes out the window in favor of tidiness and conformity. The everyday landscape denies that plants are "living, breathing organisms," Burrell says.

To return to the reluctant gardener, then, what are quick and easy steps to end front-yard embarassment, to bring the home plot in line with the neighborhood? Tidy up, mow the lawn, put in bright flowers in beds, pin those scalped foundation plants against the foundation. The neighbors will smile with approval.

Landscape architects are trained to bring more into their thinking as they create a landscape than the typical reluctant gardener brings. Tidiness, a view of the front door, hedges on a property boundary may all end up in a landscape architect's final design. But these elements aren't the starting point.

As Joni digs into her imagination for the perfect landscape for the Sands' yard, for instance, she considers how different spaces and planes relate to each other, how to make the foreground, background, and middle ground work. She pays attention to edges and the visual impact when two edges, such as a sidewalk and a planting bed, come together. She tries to incorporate mystery or surprise to keep the landscape interesting. She can do this by controlling views, pathways, and secret niches within the landscape, creating opportunities for someone strolling through the yard suddenly to discover a hidden spot in which to enjoy a small fountain or special plants.

She uses color and texture, from plants or hardscape, to add interest. She uses contrast, putting small spaces and large spaces together in the same landscape, placing intimate seating areas within dramatic views. And she uses the views themselves. A good view, like the distant hills visible from the Sands' yard, can come from simple good luck. Then all Joni has to do is consider how to frame it or whether it should be framed at all—with walls or trees, for instance—to heighten the effect.

Landscape architects want their creations to be legible. They want people who experience a designed landscape to be able to see some logic in it, to be able to "read" the design. Some landscape architects, like Joni, want something else, too. They want their landscapes to be environmentally sensitive, to mesh with the surrounding natural areas and systems.

The Sands' front porch nags Joni. She must figure how to make it attractive and use it to signal visitors where to enter the house. The vernacular landscape cliché might call for an arching driveway, lined on either side with beds of pansies and other annuals, linked in the middle to a path to the door introduced by two columnar cypress trees. It is a cliché that binds landscapes in well-to-do neighborhoods across the country. Joni's training and creative pride call for something else.

She begins by addressing the driveway. She lays a piece of trace over the base map and sketches two gently curving lines at a far corner of the Sands' lot. The lines form a new beginning for the driveway that gives it a longer approach, directing more attention to the front of the house.

She leads the driveway to a parking area on the street-side of the house, the side overlooked by the kitchen windows. The parking area, she decides, will balloon into an oval shape and will be edged by low-growing trees that will break up any sense of formality. She points out some rectangular symbols on the trace sketch. "These guys are cars," she says. "So you could just randomly park between the trees, and the trees would be growing right out of this chipped stone" that surfaces the parking area.

Next she considers how to get from the parking area to the front door. She designs a path that would deliver a visitor from parking level to the front porch steps. Four posts or a small arbor—at this point she is unsure which—could create the feel of a gateway on the path. She considers the porch steps, the porch itself, and the plantings leading to the front door. The plantings beside the porch and the steps could be "real Mediterranean kind of gray puffy things," she says.

She has thought about other paths leading through the landscape and into distant portions of the yard; she has the Sands' two children in mind. The paths will ultimately link together, "so it's like they have this circular plaything going." she says. She moves her sketching pencil to the large, flat open space in front of the house. "This might be a native meadow that they could choose to mow," she says. There is a spot for a pool and a pool house behind the house and an area that would be perfect for a kitchen garden. There might be a raised patio with room for a dining table near the pool. Another small seating area and a water feature might decorate the space outside the sunroom, and beyond that, the old cement slab could be dressed up into a fine sports court. There is room for so much. Having been handed the task of creating an ideal landscape, Joni, like most landscape architects, drafts a preliminary plan, knowing that her clients might ultimately decide not to incorporate every element. At this point, though, her job is to alert them to the possibilities, not restrict their options.

As she talks, Joni sketches in the paths and porches and features with light blue pencil. The pencil won't show up in photocopying, so using it allows her to change her mind. Before the day is over, she will have to commit herself to her ideas and begin outlining the blue penciled areas in ink.

She lays her pencil aside and leans over the increasingly busy base map and scans the newly sketched ideas. "It's hard," she finally says about this effort to put her design ideas on paper. The most basic elements are in, though, so she figures she has made a good start. She breaks for lunch.

III

WHAT EXACTLY IS A LANDSCAPE? IS IT A gorgeous natural setting of woodland and meadow? Is it a nearly open lot like the Sands' homestead? Or is it that nest of ratty-looking weeds in a suburban back yard that, with a little squinting, looks almost like a lawn?

Most standard dictionary definitions link the word "landscape" first to the natural scenery. It is defined as an awesome vista or a painting of an awesome vista. Implied in these definitions is the idea that a landscape doesn't involve people except as passive (and awestruck) viewers. As a secondary definition, dictionaries mention the aspect of landscape that involves human intervention. "Landscape," they say, is also a verb that means to contour land and move around plants to *improve* the scene, whether it be a natural scene or a garden. This second definition, with its use of a word as value-laden as "improve," is muddled by a list of questions. Is clearing a forest to create a meadow an improvement? If the result of contouring and planting is a scene uglier than what was once there, is it still landscape or merely a desecration?

Some scholars don't include natural landscapes within their definitions of landscape. They limit landscape to land that humans have had some part in changing. Yosemite Valley, with its long history of human occupation and all that it entails, would be a landscape. A little-known canyon in South Dakota's Black Hills would not. This limitation seems to reflect a particularly aggressive strain of anthropocentrism. It implies that a place is not a place until a person has embedded a heavy footprint. It also tends to separate the world into a kind of them-and-us situation, with the "them" being the places that people haven't yet changed and the "us" being the places that people have changed. Is someone among these scholars keeping a scorecard, adding points to the "us" column as humans bulldoze their way into natural areas?

Michael Laurie, a landscape architect, scholar, and author of one of the standard landscape-architecture texts, offers a more objective definition of landscape. He defines landscape as land that is "described or seen in terms of its physiographic and environmental characteristics. Landscape varies according to these characteristics and according to the historical impact of man on it."

Laurie's definition offers a common-sensical approach. It recognizes that landscape isn't a static measure of taste or values. Terms like "improve" have no place in this definition of landscape. Land that is expansive, moderately hilly, covered by a lush forest of spruce and pine, and has never been touched by human hands is landscape. Land that is flat as Sheetrock, confined by an aging wooden fence, and covered with weeds imitating lawn is landscape. A city plaza paved in Italian marble and with nary a plant in sight is landscape. The median strip on a boulevard is landscape—or at least part of a landscape. Whether it is natural or created, whether it is haphazard or carefully designed, a landscape is a landscape is a landscape. And all the landscape types, created or natural, professionally designed or not designed, affect people.

Landscape, according to Laurie, "is a reflection of dynamic, natural, and social systems." Landscape architecture, he notes, "is concerned with the planning and design of land and water for use by society on the basis of an understanding of these systems."

The profession's early founders included in their pursuit of landscape architecture a kind of progressive idealism. They saw their work as a tool for social reform and enlightenment, a way to make the world a better place for everyone, not simply the wealthy who were among their most frequent clients.

The most famous and influential of these founders, Frederick Law Olmsted, was remarkable in the way Benjamin Franklin or Thomas Jefferson was remarkable—in a different era and in a different arena. He was born in Connecticut in 1822 and spent his first forty years collecting enough experience for several lifetimes. He was a farmer intent on reforming farming practice; a newspaper columnist who blasted slavery in three books about his pre-Civil War travels in the South; a magazine editor devoted to intellectual discourse; and a park superintendent. He had traveled to China and through Europe. Above all, he was a reformer. Everything he did seemed to be linked to the goal of social reform, reflecting his deep sense of moral obligation to do work that would, he believed, improve other people's lives.

In 1857, he teamed up with landscape designer Calvert Vaux to compete for the job of creating a new park in Manhattan. Together, Vaux and Olmsted coined the term "landscape architect" to describe what they were as they proceeded to plan and oversee construction of New York's Central Park. Long before it was built, Olmsted believed Central Park would have a profound impact that would carry beyond Manhattan's borders. It would be, he said, "the first real park made in this country" and he predicted that its success would be a keystone in the development of the country's art and culture. It was only one of many predictions Olmsted would live to see come true.

Over the next forty years, Olmsted focused on landscape architecture and was involved in hundreds of significant projects, including massive park and city planning projects in Boston, Buffalo, and Brooklyn. He laid the philosophical foundation for the National Park Service, which his son, Frederick Law Olmsted, Jr., ultimately helped create. In all this, he continued to be the reformer.

"He intended his parks to be public institutions of recreation and popular education that would demonstrate the viability of the republican experiment in America," writes Olmsted scholar Charles Beveridge in his book *Frederick Law Olmsted: Designing the American Landscape.* "In the rest of his work, designing residential communities and institutions and planning the grounds of single-family homes, he sought to promote the values of community and domesticity that he had earlier defined as the mainstays of civilization."

Olmsted's greatest inspiration for landscape came from scenes he viewed as a youth during family outings in the Connecticut Valley, and landscapes and parks he saw while traveling in Europe, especially England. He was not a naturalist and his understanding of what we call ecology—the interrelationship between organisms and among organisms and their environment—was limited by the times and his own interest. Nevertheless, in eschewing certain conventions of garden design, he exhibited a deep sensitivity to nature. He rejected the contrivance of brilliant displays of large flowers in distinctive beds that reflected nothing of the way the nature he knew looked. He favored instead the delicate subtleties presented by varying shades of shrubs and trees. He actually cared little about plants as such. For him, they were like paint on a palette. He used what would give him the effect he wanted. That effect, more often than not, required using plants native to the local area.

The effect Olmsted typically wanted included curving walkways, rocky stream banks with dense foliage, long views of meadows leading to clusters of trees. He was largely self-taught and was clearly inspired by some of his recent predecessors in landscape design in the United States and England, people such as Andrew Jackson Downing and Humphrey Repton. They urged more sensitivity to local topography and natural landscapes. He mixed pastoralism and the picturesque, two elements of landscape design Olmsted saw firsthand while traveling in England. He didn't create replicas of nature, but rather interpretations based on impressions. The goal was to provide the kind of scenery he thought would help urban dwellers reflect on nature and attain a sense of tranquillity. His parks, especially, were meant simultaneously to provide recreation, level class differences, and promote health.

He was also sensitive to place. In California, at Stanford University, he proposed a landscape design and plant selection suited to a drier climate. It was an idea that his clients at that campus never really bought. They had come from the East and associated academic greatness with the lush green landscapes of New England campuses.

By the time the American Society of Landscape Architects was founded in 1899, officially establishing landscape architecture as a profession, Olmsted was already considered the father of American landscape architecture. His son, Frederick Law Olmsted, Jr., was one of the eleven architects who met to found the society.

Joni Janecki can't help but be influenced by Olmsted. No landscape architect in America is trained without reference to him or his projects. Hints of his influence seep into practically every American landscape architect's designs. Even if the landscape architect isn't consciously aware of Olmsted's influence, it is there. How can it not be? There was virtually no type of landscape project that he didn't do on a grander scale than most ever get the opportunity to do. He is to landscape architects what Shakespeare is to playwrights, Hippocrates is to physicians, George Washington is to Presidents. Even elements or ideas he didn't originate—like pastoralism—have become so linked to him that, like landscape itself, Olmsted is everywhere.

After an hour away at lunch, Joni gets back to work on the Sands plan. The rain falls harder outside and the day looks even gloomier than it did earlier. But she feels happier and a little more confident than she did when the workday began, because now the base map is no longer blank. It is starting to look like a site plan, with recognizable shapes and symbols that will add up to a landscape.

Joni lays a three-sided ruler at the place where she imagines a front porch should be and begins running the photo-blue pencil along one edge. "So here one inch equals sixteen feet. That's scale," she explains. It is a standard for a site plan like this. Later in the design process, as more detail is required, the scale gets bigger.

To indicate the walkway to the front door, the sides of the pool in the space near the kitchen's back door, a small sitting area behind the house, Joni draws a few more lines. "This is the tedious part . . . I just want to have at least a couple of straight lines."

She picks up a compass to draw circles that indicate trees. She uses the plastic template for a small square to deftly sketch a few make-believe flagstones on a pathway. Then she goes over them in freehand to round the corners and loosen up the look. Joni doesn't do hands-on drafting as much as she would like. Arthritis makes sitting for long hours over a drafting board painfully uncomfortable, and the other administrative duties that go into running a business give her little time to draw. But she will do this first round of drafting on this plan because she doesn't feel she has sufficiently developed the ideas for Michael or Robin to draw under her direction. It wouldn't be efficient to put the plan into the computer now, either.

She turns her attention to the driveway and parking area again. She wants to make it functional and beautiful, a hard thing to do with any parking area. So she comes back to it many times through the day. Now she thinks that it should be round rather than oval. She begins sketching, then reconsiders. She pulls out a stray piece of paper and begins working some simple math on it. The circle is out. She will do an ellipse instead. Ellipses are hard to draw, "but they're a really beautiful form," she says as she works numbers on the Fibonacci sequence to help determine the dimensions of the ellipse before she draws.

Leonardo Fibonacci, also known as Leonardo of Pisa (as in Leaning Tower), lived during the late twelfth and early thirteenth centuries. He was among the earliest serious mathematicians in Europe. He introduced the mathematics of India and Arabia to Europeans, as well as some algebra, for which untold generations of junior high students have not been grateful.

Among the interesting algebraic equations Fibonacci introduced is one that produces a sequence in which the numbers are related to each other through addition. For instance, the first number in the sequence is 1. The second number is 2, the result of adding 1 + 1. The third number is 3, the result of adding 1 + 2. The fourth number is 5, the result of adding the second number, 2, and the third number, 3. The fifth number is 8, the result of adding the third number and the fourth number. And so on, so that the sequence goes 1, 2, 3, 5, 8, 13, 21, 34, 55, 89, etc.

Fibonacci's sequence was just interesting when he introduced it. But since then scientists have found that it expresses a pattern that appears in biology and genetics. Architects, artists, landscape architects, and people who make index cards and rugs have found that the Fibonacci numbers when used in sequential pairs express dimensions that are particularly pleasing to the eye. A three-by-five rectangle just feels better than a three-by-four rectangle.

"I think fifty-five feet would be right if I followed this Fibonacci thing," Joni concludes, and then pulls out a piece of trace to do a test run on an ellipse that would be fifty-five feet long and thirty-four feet wide. It looks right to her, and she does the drawing again on the plan, still working in photo-blue pencil. She draws some small circles around the edge of the ellipse to indicate trees. She doesn't know what kind of tree yet, and before she considers the issue, her attention jumps to another part of the plan, just as it has been hopscotching across the base map all day.

"That's a big planter," she notes about the area she has marked near the front porch. "Maybe there should be more usable space." She ponders the entire yard, seeing beyond the white paper with the blue lines to some creative place in her mind where this landscape has fuller form. "Guess we'll plant it, bring it back to a little habitat. They could have a pond, a little wildlife pond." Then, silently, she concentrates on the plan, drawing lines, symbols, and pathways here and there.

Joni sits straight up for a view of the whole plan at once,

then slumps a little, looking almost defeated. "I feel like I don't really have a lot of meaning in here right now, heartfelt deep meaning . . . There's nothing that says this is what this place is to me yet. And that's pretty unusual," she complains. "I can see it and I can see what it looks like, but I don't really know what it is. It would help to know that, I think, especially as I go along." A moment more and she is back to drawing, concluding with resignation that maybe the meaning will emerge on its own.

Lyle Lovett croons on the stereo. Judy Titchenal, the firm's part-time bookkeeper and office manager, who brings a soothing aura of hip motherliness to the office, selected the music. She lightly sways to it as she goes through bills and invoices at her desk in the main room. Joni seems oblivious to the sound. Robin works on the park plan at her corner table. Michael is home in bed with a bad back today. Occasionally, the women trade observations or chat as they work. The mood is mellow industriousness.

"We're into having a good, comfortable space," Joni says about her office. Joni has never really worked in what she would call an uptight landscape architecture firm, the kind of place where there is a formal reception area, a hierarchy of space, where some people have windows and some people don't, depending on their level in the practice. In those firms—usually much larger than Joni's shop—even the look of the work reflects the rigid, no-nonsense management. The work is polished to the point of slickness. Joni describes it as "very clipped, a lot of colored markers and not colored pencils. Sharp. Crisp. Sort of like tract-home advertising, which doesn't appeal to me."

Joni's favorite landscape architect, Roberto Burle Marx, was notorious for his gregarious warmth and the casual atmosphere in his office. The Brazilian designer's Rio de Janeiro office was once described as having "a very unceremonial atmosphere." A bevy of assistants, associates, partners, and visitors flowed in and out of his office through the workday, as Burle Marx reviewed designs, talked on the phone, or broke into an aria (he had an operatic voice).

Burle Marx, who died in 1995 after more than sixty years in the field, was not formally trained as a landscape architect. He had studied art and had a complementary career as a painter. Like the best landscape architects, Joni explains, "he could express himself in an architectural way and an artistic way. He was one person who could create that inside/outside feeling without being too gardeny."

His designs were bold and had a sense of sharp-edged whimsy. Like other landscape architects before and after him, Burle Marx used plants as a painter would use paint. But where a designer like Olmsted paid less attention to the plants' species than to their visual affect, Burle Marx paid equal attention to both. He used heavy serpentine lines and straight-edged geometric shapes to create landscapes that heightened the striking fluid shapes of Brazil's native plants. Seen from above, his landscapes curved and flowed in ways reminiscent of Brazil's Amazonian rivers and forests.

Burle Marx was a noted plantsman and, like Olmsted, a conservationist. He introduced the native plants of Brazil, including its fantastic Amazonian rain-forest flora, to urban Brazilians, whose tastes had tended toward European design, with tulips and other temperate-climate plants in their gardens. He knew intimately the plants he was working with, having grown many of them in his own nursery. He counted other plant enthusiasts among his large group of friends and explored Amazonian plant life with botanists. And he advocated the protection of the rain forest.

Burle Marx had an international reputation, but what was striking about him was his national standing in Brazil. He was a popular guy recognized by the man on the street as much as by the landscape aficionado. There is no landscape architect in the last fifty years who has achieved equal stature in the United States.

But not all the 1,700 projects he completed in his lifetime could be described as inviting. Some of his largest, including work he did in Brasilia as it was becoming a city, overpower as much as the sterile buildings they were designed to accompany. Some, to Joni's eye, look almost uninhabitable. Even the nicest office atmosphere doesn't guarantee that a designer will create inviting landscapes.

"That is one talented guy," Judy remarks from her desk in the other room.

"Burle?" Joni asks, not raising her eyes from the base map.

"What?"

"Who?"

"Lyle."

"Oh."

IV

LANDSCAPE ARCHITECTS DIVIDE THE PARTS OF a landscape into two basic categories: hardscape and softscape. Hardscape is nonliving. It includes sidewalks, pathways, patios, curbs, swimming pools, and fountains. Furnishings are in a subcategory of hardscape. They include picnic tables, bicycle racks, benches, lightposts, tree-well grates, and other items that have both decorative and functional uses.

Softscape is the life of the landscape. It is the plants, or, as many landscape architects say, the plant material. The plants, their species, how they are placed and how they are maintained, can be fluid and changing. They can soften the hard edges of a landscape, brighten or darken a corner, or reinforce some sentiment expressed by the hardscape, its rigidity or lyricism. Plants can complement or contrast with the hardscape. If you think of a created landscape as a living organism, the hardscape is its skeleton. The plants are its heart and soul.

Three main groups determine what plants we see each day in the built landscape: the people who design the landscapes, the people who grow and sell plants, and the people who buy the designs and the plants. Sometimes these groups overlap. Clearly, landscape architects are not the only ones responsible for the plants we see. But their impact is huge if you count how many plants they include in their designs. Researchers who tried to quantify the impact surveyed landscape architects in Georgia. The researchers determined that in that state alone the demand for plants for landscape architect-designed projects accounted for more than 42 percent of the value of all the plants grown in Georgia nurseries in a single year. Put another way, those landscape architects were worth about $85 million in business to the state's nurseries.

Many contemporary landscape architects have a reputation in the plant industry—among horticulturists, growers, and landscape installers—as having little real interest in plants. Indeed, some of landscape architecture's most celebrated stars during the thirty years after World War II indulged in hardscape and paid little attention to plants or ecology. Stark landscapes with hard edges and lots of concrete and stone typified this group's best-known work. Their approach left an imprint on subsequent generations. As one plant-oriented landscape architect recently told *Landscape Architecture* magazine, "It seems that sometimes landscape architects are embarrassed that we have something to do with plants."

As part of their training, landscape architects must learn about plants. But how much they learn depends on which school they go to and on their own interests. Once they leave school, how much they care or continue to learn about plants depends almost entirely on their own interest.

Plant enthusiasts in the nursery industry (and not everyone in the nursery industry is a plant enthusiast) often complain that landscape architects have a list of Top 40 plants from which they never deviate. If they used masses of yellow daylilies successfully on one project, then ten years later they will still be using masses of yellow daylilies. Some landscape architects blame people in the nursery industry for hindering creativity, plant diversity, and especially regional identity. The nurseries usually provide only the plants they are convinced will make money, plants that have always been reliable sellers. Often it is the same Top 40.

What becomes commercial, successful, and then widely available in the nursery industry usually falls into an extremely narrow range. "At any given point, only a handful of plants make that cut," said J. C. Raulston, director of the North Carolina State University Arboretum in Raleigh, during an interview one fall day in 1995. A plant "has to be economic for the nursery to grow and make a profit on, which means, more or less, that it has to be very easy to propagate and very fast growing. There are few [plants] that will make it on a wide basis that don't have these two things."

Plants like yellow daylilies, which fit the economic requirements of the nursery industry, are used over and over and over again, to the point of becoming overused. Consumers, from the landscape architects' clients to those who plant their own yards, also influence what is sold by what they buy. "There are over thirty thousand cultivars of daylilies," noted Raulston, who was nationally known for his devotion to expanding the nursery industry's plant stock (he died in an automobile accident in 1996). "There's something like fifteen hundred new ones introduced annually." Yet there's one cultivar, one variety, that accounts for the majority of the daylilies sold in America. A golden-yellow one called Stella de Oro.

Why people prefer one plant over another—often a familiar plant over a new one—depends on many variables. Price and availability are two of the most important. If nurseries aren't carrying certain plants, they simply aren't available. Ease of care may play a role, too. Media exposure can boost interest in a plant. Magazine or newspaper articles or a mention by a radio gardening personality can increase a plant's popularity. One nursery consultant says that if doyenne of tasteful homes Martha Stewart says good things about a plant on one of her television shows, it will quickly sell out in areas where the program airs.

David Fross, a nurseryman who specializes in growing California native plants, has thought a lot about attachments to specific plants. All of us, he concludes, come to our gardens with a narrative voice linking our present to our history. A woman may remember the fall leaf color in Ohio from her childhood and forever after yearn for the American sweet gum tree and its brilliant fall displays. When she moves to a different part of the country, say New Mexico or Montana, she plants a sweet gum.

People are also influenced by fashion. Clothing shoppers are influenced by store window displays, magazine fashion layouts, and advertisements. Plant shoppers, too, are influenced by ads and the plant world's equivalent of a window display: the landscape. Consider a neighborhood drive-through bank that has a strip of standard lawn with a birch tree, daylilies and impatiens. A person comes by and sees those plants. Then he or she goes to the garden center and sees them in the garden center. "And it just reinforces itself, on and on," Fross observes. But if you start getting some interesting things in the drive-through and people come by and see something new and exciting, "maybe two percent of them are going to go down to the local garden center and say, 'What's the plant in the front of—'and they'll say, 'I want one of those.' "

For Joni, plants are the landscape ingredients that give her the best opportunity to link people with the natural environment. They are the ecological basis of a design, the means for building discrete communities that, though she admits they can't always mimic nature, might at least recall remnants of nature. Joni likes imagining how different plants will look in a landscape. She likes considering their leaf shape, color, texture, and aroma. Learning about and selecting plants is one of the entertaining parts of landscape architecture for her. It is also one of the parts that can awaken a client's tastes and attachments, the narrative that Fross talks about.

Sometimes a client's desire for certain plants can be so strong a landscape architect has to put aside her own tastes or even her informed judgment. Joni tries to remember, especially with residential landscapes, that her job is to help people arrive at their dream landscape. Sometimes that means including in a design plants that don't make the most sense to her. For instance, when one client decided that amid a mostly native California landscape she wanted to plant a bed of bearded irises, the request was almost startling. It was comparable to someone in Georgia deciding to plant a few barrel cacti on the edge of a pine forest. With every plan she designs, Joni expects to have to do a certain amount of educating. She has to help clients who don't know about native plants or natural landscapes to learn to appreciate their value. Sometimes the education works better than others. Joni tried to talk her client out of the irises, but the client would not be moved. So Joni did what she could to make sure the client got irises that would bloom well—she took her to a specialty nursery to buy $1,200 worth of the plant.

Most of the time, a client's passion for a particular plant is harmless. Sometimes, though, one person's enthusiasm for a plant leads to nearly disastrous consequences for the wildlands. What looks good within a garden's gates can become a noxious weed outside.

The most common definition of a weed is a plant that is growing where you don't want it to grow. It is usually a plant that takes advantage of some soil disturbance—a freshly spaded garden, the wake of new construction, the impact of hundreds of cattle hooves. Most people consider weeds unattractive. Objectively speaking, dandelions have charming yellow blooms, and some parts are edible. To most gardeners in America, though, they are a pest, because dandelions are aggressive and overtake what gardeners *want* to grow, the things they plant.

What about rosebushes? Few people consider the ornamental plants that grace gardens to be weeds. Some plants may be harder to train to stay in their part of the garden, but even then we don't call them weeds. Delinquents maybe, but not weeds. Yet as ecologists, botanists, and others have intensified their examination of our country's wildlands in the last two decades, they have found that a lot of plants that people import from other countries, and even other regions of the United States are taking over.

From the Sierra Nevada to the Everglades, from the Ozarks to the Adirondacks, exotic pests are creating a plant kingdom version of destruction by domination, forcing native plants out. They are slashing the local biological diversity, reducing local plant communities from dozens of different members to just a few. Sometimes they become so aggressive that nothing but that exotic plant grows. These plants are changing the wildlands environment, turning the plant equivalent of colorful, sensual villages into bland tracts of look-alike developments. The worst among them are nearly impossible to eradicate.

There are sections of California and Arizona desert, for instance, where the local plants have been overrun by certain types of tamarisk. Commonly called salt cedar, this flowering tree native to Asia, Europe, and Africa is especially adapted to tolerate drought and heavy winds. Settlers started planting this pretty, hardy tree throughout the Southwest in the early 1800s to provide shade and act as windbreak. But the very things that make the tree so hardy and adaptable to harsh conditions proved to be its greatest drawbacks. It grows like crazy. A single tree produces hundreds of thousands of seeds each year, and once a seedling gets established, it can grow up to a foot per month. A mature salt cedar and its offspring have no respect for neighboring plants. They settle into creek-side plant communities and drink groundwater down to the last drop, leaving nothing for anyone or anything else. Salt cedar even exudes a substance that makes the soil around its base too salty for some animals.

A network of scientists who are compiling a comprehensive list of North American flora have determined that about 18,000 plant species are found in the wild spaces of North America outside of Mexico. Estimates vary, but at least 3,000 of those wildland plants are exotic, introduced to the region after Europeans started settling America. Some of the exotics came in as accidental hitchhikers on sheep hooves and in imported seed bags and plant pots. But many escaped from intentional cultivation to grow on undeveloped lands. The ratio between native plants and introduced plants in the wild varies from state to state. One study estimates, for example, that more than one-third of the plant species in New York State's natural areas are introduced. In California, about one-sixth are non-native. The states that were settled first, where people have had the longest time to have an impact, typically have the greatest proportion of introduced species in their wildlands.

Not all the introduced plant species in the wild spread as aggressively as mold on white bread, and nobody knows exactly how many are actually damaging the wildlands. However, a few statistics give a hint. In California, for instance, there are about a thousand species of exotic non-natives in the wild, and of those, at least seventy are considered pests by weed watchers. To varying degrees, exotic pest-plant problems are known all over the country. Florida and Hawaii, with tropical climates that make life easy for green things that grow fast, have been especially burdened by escaped plants pushing out wild ones. A survey of 246 National Park Service superintendents around the country found that more than half ranked non-native plants as a moderate to major problem in their parks.

The sad twist is that many of the known exotic pest plants were introduced with good intentions. Often the plants were no problem for decades and stayed in the garden. Then a few started creeping into natural areas. Or sometimes well-intentioned government agencies actually introduced them into wild areas long before anyone understood the full impact of exotic pest plants.

Kudzu, the vine that has transformed whole forests from collections of trees into hulking, brooding green masses that look as if they stepped out of some ghost story, is the classic example of a federal agency's plant promotion gone wrong. The Soil Conservation Service promoted this Asian plant by the millions in the late 1930s as a means to hold soil in place. Today kudzu is a weedy disaster, covering and killing thousands of acres of natural growth from Texas to Long Island. In kitschy novelty stores in Atlanta, tourists snap up T-shirts imprinted with the words: "Kudzu—The Plant That Ate The South."

Other well-meaning state and federal agencies have wreaked havoc following forest and brush fires. They commonly seed burned areas with non-native grasses, particularly if erosion of the burned areas might threaten private property. These grasses end up becoming pest plants that not only push out natives but are even worse fire hazards themselves because they become dry and are highly flammable in summer.

Highway departments around the country are notorious

for providing gateways into the wild for exotic plants. One of the first things these departments do after building a road is landscape the roadside areas that were disturbed during construction. Until the 1920s, according to one study by John Harrington, a landscape-architecture professor at the University of Wisconsin, roadside landscaping was restricted by technology and money. Road builders just let whatever already grew on the roadside continue growing. Usually that meant that local, native plants moved in and re-created the natural landscape that had been there before the bulldozers went to work.

Then herbicides and lawnmowers were invented and improved. Enter high-maintenance roadside landscapes consisting of lawn-worthy exotic grasses, accented with equally exotic shrubs and trees. In California, for instance, the state's transportation department included in roadside landscapes pampas grass, Hottentot fig, and eucalyptus trees, three plants that today are common pest plants in natural areas.

In the 1970s, as energy prices and water and maintenance costs rose, road-building agencies looked for ways to save landscaping money. By the 1980s, various highway departments, particularly in the Midwest, began consciously including native plants in roadside landscapes. Nevertheless, most continue to be dominated by non-native plants—there isn't enough money to go back and redo all the landscapes along older roads. Even if there were, interest in promoting native landscape varies from agency to agency and from person to person.

Individual gardeners and the nursery industry also share some blame for disastrous plantings. In the mid-1800s, a

Santa Barbara nurseryman introduced pampas grass to U.S. gardeners after importing it from Argentina. A shaggy tower of sharp-edged blades and giant, feathery white plumes that can reach a dozen feet high, pampas grass charmed plant lovers. Its plumes became adornments for greeting cards and the plant itself became common, especially in California gardens. Today it is a major problem, invading oak woodland, coastal sage, wetlands, and other areas throughout Southern and central California. Each feathery plume sends out thousands of seeds, many of which successfully anchor in even the smallest patch of exposed soil. Pampas plants spring from the steep roadside cliffs along the famous winding Pacific Coast Highway near Big Sur. Wedding celebrants in that area occasionally strap plumes to their car antennas, naïvely helping the plant spread its seeds.

Nursery owners and gardeners brought thorny multiflora roses to the United States from Asia in the early 1800s. A hundred years later, federal and state agencies, including the Soil Conservation Service, promoted the plant in a handful of Eastern states as a great way to control erosion and feed wildlife. By the 1950s, it had a reputation for running wild and pushing out just about any other plant in its way, including farm plants. Birds that eat the multiflora's abundant seeds helped it spread across the country. Today several Midwestern and Eastern states list it as a noxious weed.

And the list goes on. Brazilian pepper trees and Australian melaleuca trees are just two of a long list of exotic pest plants that are strangling Florida, particularly its wetlands. Purple loosestrife, a pretty flowering plant native to Europe, has been a garden favorite for two hundred years in the United

States. It has also become a pest in all but a handful of states, aggressively crowding natives out of wetland habitats.

Logging, grazing, and development have also taken their toll on the country's native plants. All this adds up to a loss of biological diversity that makes an ecosystem more vulnerable to assaults from cyclical catastrophic events like droughts and floods. Introducing invasive pest plants into an already weakened ecosystem is like throwing a flu virus into a roomful of people who already have pneumonia. It almost guarantees that not everyone will come out of the room alive.

Ecological damage is just one problem posed by exotic pest plants. Another is economic harm. Exotic pest plants cost the public millions of dollars each year by clogging waterways, creating fire hazards, and promoting erosion. It costs millions more to get rid of them. The now defunct Congressional Office of Technology Assessment estimated in a comprehensive 1993 report on non-indigenous pests that, between 1906 and 1991, just fifteen non-native pest plants had caused about $603 million in losses. The report also estimated that in the future three plants alone—melaleuca, purple loosestrife, and witchweed—would cost more than $4.5 billion.

There is no single method to eradicate pest plants. Generally, too, the known methods are imperfect and people charged with eliminating the pests are often left to choose among undesirable options. Doing nothing will let the pest spread while it kills out the native species and the animals that depend upon them. Applying herbicides has to be done with special care because the herbicides that kill weeds can also kill native plants and animals. Even simple hard labor, pulling and digging weeds out, isn't ideal. These mechanical methods, according to ecologist and weed specialist John Randall, disturb the soil and destroy vegetation, providing a toehold for more weeds. Finally, introducing biological control agents, such as a plant-eating insect, carries the risk that the agent will get out of hand, feeding on everything, not just the target weed. "In addition, once established, biological control agents cannot be recalled and may undergo genetic or behavioral changes that allow them to feed on new hosts," cautions Randall.

The only sure way to deal with wildland weeds is not to introduce them in the first place. For Joni, that means never recommending plants that are known wildland pests, even for landscapes that aren't adjacent to natural areas. As the old English proverb has it (or surely would have it if old proverb makers had known about the weed problem), an ounce of prevention is worth at least a pound of herbicide.

Fortunately for Dennis Sands—and Joni—the monkey puzzle tree he covets is not a known pest. As Joni puts the finishing touches on the first draft of the Sands' new landscape plan, she contemplates where the tree would look best. As she recalls, there already is a very young one in a far corner of the Sands' yard. But now, many weeks and hundreds of miles from her Montecito visit, Joni has second thoughts about whether the corner tree is really a monkey puzzle or one of two related trees, a Norfolk pine or a bunya bunya. She pulls a plant book off a shelf and looks for descriptions. All three trees have branches that spread in distinctive layers, none is native to California, and all require regular watering, get very tall, and need a lot of space. The book's information is frustratingly sketchy, and she looks pensive as she turns back to the plan. She doesn't want the new tree to dominate the landscape, but it is one of only a few requests the Sands have made, so its placement is critical.

She stares at the plan, moving her pencil millimeters above the paper, before she settles it on a spot at the back of the house. The tree would fit in that spot, she figures. Then, as she studies the house layout, she realizes that from there the tree would be in clear view of Dennis's office window. He could enjoy a view of it while he works. It's a perfect place, she decides, and draws a circle for the monkey puzzle tree.

By late afternoon, Joni has drawn in most of the plan and begun hardlining it, running permanent ink over the nearly invisible light-blue pencil. Robin, a tall, slender young woman with short blond hair and lively eyes, wanders in and looks over Joni's shoulder at the day's work.

"Oooo. Nice," Robin coos.

The words are like the sound of a motorboat to a desert-island castaway. Joni's doubts begin to fade and she becomes animated. "I was just getting to a point where I was going to do this," she says, indicating the ragged symbols for trees around the ellipse. Then she sweeps her pen, a makeshift pointer, around to different spots on the plan and describes them in shorthand. "This is maybe water. This could be flagstone with just crushed stone in between. And this could be water here. Then this is a spa or hot tub or sauna."

Robin follows the pen from one feature to another. "I like this whole interaction, and the proportions look right."

The first critique is going well and Joni is clearly relieved. Then she shares some of the ideas she is less certain about, indirectly soliciting advice from her colleague. She starts with the nagging parking area.

"When you get out here to this front thing . . . coming into the courtyard, maybe these are orange trees or something. Something that doesn't get too big but that you can park under and that smells good."

"Oh, yeah," Robin agrees.

So far, so good.

"You can drive in and park under the trees . . . But it would be that kind of thing." Joni draws in a couple of rectangles representing cars to illustrate the parking pattern. She moves her pen to the new stepped pathway from the parking area. "Then here have some kind of arbor to make this an entrance. But I wasn't sure if this might be looking too—"

"Too formal?"

"Yeah," Joni says with a laugh.

Robin and Joni are both of a generation of designers who favor practical and natural over formal and rigid. Formality can be expressed in clipped hedges and hard edges, or it can be expressed in symmetry. If everything is lined up in even amounts, if everything fits into equal parts on an axis, then it smacks of formality. And they both know that neither Abbe nor Dennis is interested in living in a formal garden.

"If you use orange trees, I don't think you would feel that, because you have all the multi-stem," Robin offers. "You don't get the single-stem thing that makes the rigid edges. Multi-stem would make a big difference."

However, orange trees aren't native to California. The generally accepted definition of native plant in the United States is one that grew wild in a place before European settlers arrived. Spanish missionaries planted California's first orange trees in the early 1800s. Joni isn't a native-plant purist, though, and for orange trees she can be flexible. "It smells really nice to go into a courtyard of orange trees," she says. Besides, she likes the idea of fruit trees. "There's just something nice about picking your own fruit."

The two women chat about the size of the ellipse and whether it will be big enough for adequate parking. They agree to put the trees on the outside of the ellipse, to provide a bit more space. They move to the driveway. Is it wide enough? Yes. But how will it look?

Joni likes the old-fashioned driveways that have two tracks of concrete where the car wheels ride. Robin agrees. "And then you have little baby tears or grasses in the middle." But almost as soon as they agree, they reject the idea when they realize that once the driveway hits the parking area they couldn't continue the split without sending half a car down one side of the ellipse and the other half down the other side. The image sets off a round of laughter. They decide instead to recommend a brick driveway with grasses or other plants between the bricks.

They talk about a kitchen garden, a back porch with broad curved steps, an arbor outside the sunroom, and the views from inside that sunroom that someday will overlook a swimming pool and a narrow stream and tiny pond. They talk about where people will sit, where they will play, where they will walk, where they will find the surprises like the secret niche with the tiny fountain. They talk about the meadow in front of the house, created in an oval shape. Suddenly Joni realizes that the meadow of wildflowers and native grasses, an unconscious nod to Olmsted, is a key link in the plan's layout.

"I love that it is pretty much a formal meadow, and yet you don't really feel it's formalized," Robin tells her. "The architecture and the lines are formal, but the visual picture that I get isn't formal, it's soft."

"Yeah!" Joni is nearly giddy. "That's the idea."

"It's California trying to do Cape Cod. California trying to do that rigid box look with the formal lines and everything, but doing it California-style," Robin continues, "much more responsible and politically correct."

The plan has found its meaning.

Robin wanders back to her desk as Joni calls out a thank you to her. It is almost 5:30 and Joni is tired. She has finished the hardest part. The main ideas are down in their symbolic lines, squares, and circles. But there is still a lot to be done before she can roll the plan into a mailing tube and send it to the Sands. She must label everything on the plan, finish putting in details such as the front gate and the secret fountain. Then she will make photocopies and mark one copy in colored pencil for the Sands. She will make giant photocopies instead of diazo prints, the sort of blue-lined drawings—

blueprints—typically used by architects. The diazo process makes the paper unrecyclable and resistant to adding penciled corrections or notes.

Usually, Joni would sit down with a client to present and explain the finished first version of the plan. She would bring along photographs of other gardens or features to help illustrate what she envisions. She would be able to see and gauge the client's reaction firsthand. She would collect comments and then return to her office to do a final plan and provide a plant list. But since the Sands live a half day's drive or a $200 airplane flight away, Joni won't be in Montecito for the plan's unveiling. "We understand one another pretty well," she reasons. "Also, they're pretty sophisticated at reading plans." She will catch up with them by phone to answer any questions and receive comments.

Joni stretches and decides to quit for the day. "I wish I was finished, so I could send it to them," she says. She plans to finish it tomorrow and get it into the overnight express mail. She leaves the plan, pencils, pens, and other tools in their place on the table, ready to take up again in the morning. Then she gives one more long look to her work.

"I feel good about it," she says, then adds, "I hope they like it—I think they'll like it—but they've got to live with it. They've got to look at it and feel like 'Wow! This is headed where I want to go.' "

V

PHIL KOENIG CLIMBS BEHIND THE STEERING wheel of an electric golf cart and shifts it into reverse. "We'll try to get in at least nine holes today," he says, barely restraining a Cheshire cat-like grin. This cart has never been within a driving wood's range of a golf course. Its motoring duties are all work, no pleasure. Phil uses it to save time and energy as he hurries across the grounds of computer giant Hewlett-Packard Company's main headquarters. For more than twelve years, he has helped oversee the care and management of the landscape here—forty-six acres of asphalt, concrete, plants, and buildings.

He swings the cart away from its resting spot outside a delivery entrance and speeds past rows and columns of parked cars. The air is chilly, the sky variously blue and gray. Phil stops the cart in front of a two-story building that probably looked like cutting-edge architecture in the 1950s and 1960s. Now it has a decidedly institutional, sterile feel. Its exterior has the earlier period's requisite color scheme of tan and turquoise. Tan for the concrete block, turquoise for bands of colored panels that meet rows of windows. Whole walls look like glass and metal grid paper. A tan sidewalk hugs the edge of the building, and asphalt stretches from there. Six slender trees planted in islands of hard-packed dirt provide the only break between the sidewalk and the asphalt.

Phil, a husky man in his forties, points toward the trees. "These are Platanus racemosa, the worst possible tree to plant here," he explains. They predate his arrival at HP and are probably close to thirty years old, if not older. But their trunks are barely as big around as a lumberjack's forearm. The trees are natives, commonly called either California or Western sycamores. Their natural habitat is along streams and in canyons where they can drive their taproots deep and find water even in the driest season. They are used widely in created landscapes that have space for them to grow to their full hundred-foot height. The plantings here, though, haven't worked. The soil above their roots is tightly compacted and covered with suffocating concrete. They don't have the room they need to spread, and in their weakened state they keep getting hit by anthracnose, a fungus that causes the tree leaves to drop prematurely. Then new leaves grow, get the fungus, and drop again. "We have one guy and all he does is rake these leaves up all year," Phil complains. It is a gloomy scene, and the people who work behind the windows that look out onto it have made it known that they want a change.

The company's managers have dubbed this Building 6, a plain and practical title for a plain and practical edifice. Its corner touches Building 4, which touches Building 2. The three buildings together are arranged so that their outside edges suggest sawteeth or a stack of full and partial Zs. They are among the earliest buildings erected here after Hewlett-Packard made Stanford Research Park in Palo Alto its corporate headquarters in 1954.

For about thirty-five years, these buildings were home to various manufacturing works that helped produce the scientific instruments and computing equipment that made HP a multibillion-dollar international corporation. The emphasis was on utility when these buildings were put up. There had to be plenty of room to roll heavy equipment and products in and out of them. There had to be handy spots for storing chemicals, other nearby spots for trash Dumpsters. Landscape that went beyond the bare minimum didn't seem necessary or practical.

As the rest of the Palo Alto site grew and more buildings were constructed, the company—sometimes Phil himself—put in new landscapes and thousands of plants. There are magnolias from the Southeast, Monterey pines from coastal California, pistache trees from China, and dozens of different sorts of shrubs, flowers, and grasses. Some buildings are surrounded by stands of pines among flows of flawless lawn and leafy groundcover. Some are framed by low-lying collections of native grasses and ornamental shrubs. But through the years the landscape at Buildings 2, 4, and 6 has remained minimal.

Then came the folks from the company's Integrated Circuit Business Division (ICBD). While looking for ways to streamline and cut costs, Hewlett-Packard executives decided to close some of the company's offices in the San Francisco

Bay Area. The people who work in ICBD were assigned to move from their Santa Clara site about twenty miles south of Palo Alto to Building 6 at company headquarters. Since nearly sixty percent of the people affected would face a longer commute each day, the news wasn't entirely welcome. Employee enthusiasm for the move dropped further as a few of the ICBD workers started checking out their future Palo Alto home and sending horror stories back to their colleagues.

The building space earmarked for ICBD looked dungeonous. It was dark and the floors were concrete. Pipes were exposed. It had been a manufacturing site, so it looked nothing like a modern corporate office with comfortable desks and chairs, carpet, and good lighting. Then there was the view. It was ugly with a capital U. In no time, ICBD members started worrying that their new home would be a dump.

Company managers assured the ICBD members that the Palo Alto site would be remodeled into a comfortable workplace before the move. They also promised to improve the view. The ambience of discount car lot would vanish.

Indeed, by the time the first ICBD engineers had cleaned out their Santa Clara desks and transferred to Palo Alto, the interior of Building 6 was as attractive as promised. The lighting was fine, the carpet was clean, the desks and partitions were in place. But the outside? Hello, car lot. The company's managers had not abandoned their commitment to a pleasing landscape. But their landscaping plans had stalled while they worked out critical details, like whom to hire to do the project, how much to do, and how much to spend.

Landscape is serious business in corporate America. The attitude at HP is that the buildings and the landscape are an asset. "We now manage that landscape as something that actually has monetary value," Phil says. The company figures the landscape increases their property values while it contributes aesthetic value. So HP works hard to keep its landscape in shape and its value high, even relying on high-tech computer technology to help decide where to direct its landscape-maintenance attention.

For instance, the company contracts with landscape-maintenance firms whose job it is to keep the planted areas looking healthy and attractive. It contracts with a landscape auditing firm that compiles computerized data on water use and employs infrared photography to track the health and growth of the landscape's plants. Auditing helps identify problems that the maintenance people may have missed—a weed patch or a dry section—and indicates areas that can't be maintained in the time and with the money allotted. It gives Phil quantitative data to help him make qualitative decisions about whether it's time to replace certain labor- or water-consuming plants.

Landscape is more than just a means to enhance property values, though. It also sends a message that supports or degrades a corporate image. If it is well cared for and attractive, the landscape suggests that a company is successful, attentive, high-quality. It the landscape is shoddy and unkempt, "Well," it says, "bring your business here and maybe we'll do the work right, maybe we won't." If it is formal, it suggests tradition; if it is casual or wilder or more natural-looking, it suggests sensitivity to nature. Beyond the message it sends to potential clients, landscape will also affect employees who work in the company's buildings.

When Frederick Law Olmsted devoted himself to the business of landscape architecture, and particularly park design, he did so believing that he was contributing to the public welfare by providing a natural experience for weary urbanites. Olmsted helped introduce to American culture the notion that nature and natural surroundings restore. He believed that natural scenes eased a person's mind, delighted the senses, and revitalized one's spirit. Yet it has only been since the 1970s, really, that researchers have tried to determine if there is a scientific basis for such a notion. In the 1980s and 1990s, researchers, particularly those interested in the relatively new field of environmental psychology, began to provide solid evidence that Olmsted was right.

Researchers have found that when a person has become fatigued from focusing attention on a project, exposure to a natural setting will bring relief and enhance his or her ability to focus again. In one study, participants were divided into three groups and given what scientists term "attentionally fatiguing" tasks. These are tasks such as proofreading that require intense focus and concentration. Following completion of the tasks, one group was allowed to spend forty minutes walking in a natural setting. Another group walked in an urban setting, and the third sat and read and listened to soft music. Then each group was given a proofreading test. The group that had walked among plants and other natural elements did better on the proofreading test than the other two groups.

In another study, researchers compared students who lived in dormitories with views of natural elements, such as trees, with those who lived in dormitories with views that had no natural elements. The students with the plant-rich views rated higher on tests designed to measure their ability to focus or direct their attention. Researchers have also found that just having frequent exposure to nature and natural elements, either in a wilderness setting or as expressed in a traditional garden, can improve a person's performance and ability to cope with disease. It is no wonder, then, that one of the growth areas in horticulture these days is the use of gardens and gardening as therapy in hospital settings.

For nature to restore, it doesn't have to be an expansive meadow or grand forest. Something as small as a garden plot can have restorative effects. The critical element is that, big or small, the natural elements passively help people shift their attention away from fatiguing activities and thoughts. They give the mind a break.

These research findings have special implications for employers. They suggest that a company can introduce restorative powers to the workplace simply by improving the landscape outside its windows. And maybe, with that act, a company can help improve employee happiness and productivity.

At Hewlett-Packard, nobody talks about the restorative powers of nature when they mention the asphalt view from Buildings 2, 4, and 6. They talk instead about how happy they will be to see the harsh view change.

Joni Janecki identifies as one of her strengths a lucky ability to get work. Landscape architecture is a career that might seem uncomfortably full of job interviews and the noncollegiate equivalent of entrance exams. Work doesn't just appear; it has to be won. Sometimes jobs come Joni's way from referrals by satisfied clients. Sometimes they come after she bids on projects in competition with other landscape architects. Sometimes they come from a combination of factors, including fortunate coincidence.

One evening Joni, Robin, Drew, and some friends stopped by a downtown Santa Cruz bar and music club for happy hour. HP's Phil Koenig, a nondrinking family man who spends precious little time out with the guys, was at the bar with a sailing buddy. Joni knew the sailing buddy and they all started talking. Talk turned to work and then, naturally and happily for Phil and Joni, to plants.

Sharing conversation rich with detail about leaf texture, bark color, flower shape, and watering regimen may not be everybody's idea of fun. But serious plant lovers always seem to have something to say to each other. Discovery of another plant lover leads to what is best described as horticultural bonding. In this case, it also led Joni to a new client.

Not long after that evening, Phil called and hired Joni to do a planting plan for an area at HP's Palo Alto site. The space was relatively small, only about as long and wide as a moving van trailer, but it needed something that would help hide from view a newly installed nitrogen tank. Joni submitted a plan that included native grasses, some shrubs, a few trees, and a vine. Phil liked the plan and liked working with Joni.

A few months later, HP managers in the corporate real-estate and facilities sections decided they were ready to begin landscaping the nearly barren area in front of Buildings 2, 4, and 6. A management team was formed to see the project through. Steve Shokrai, a quietly firm manager with a notable mental number-crunching talent, would oversee the whole project. Kevin Alford, a high-energy organizer, would do the day-to-day management, and Phil would assist with his plant and landscape expertise. Their first task was to find an architect, and they invited a few in for interviews. Most were big names in the Bay Area and had worked for HP before. Joni was the newcomer. During a brief interview at the company's Palo Alto site, she showed the team a résumé, talked about her work, shared a portfolio of other projects, and revealed some developing ideas she had for the HP landscape. Then she drove back to Santa Cruz and waited.

One early October day Joni received her formal invitation to compete for the technology firm's landscape. "Congratulations!" the letter from HP began, its spirit as lifting as a Publishers Clearinghouse entry form. "You have been selected to submit concepts for the upcoming HP North 1501 Site Landscaping Project." Not the most melodious title for a project, but Joni could change that later.

"We would like to see design concepts and a scope of work for a project budgeted to cost $250,000 and a project budgeted at $500,000," the letter continued. Then it listed some points the project's managers wanted her to consider as she created her design. They wanted the landscape to be a "familiar, inviting, and significant environment" that would screen the parking lots from the lower floors and also give people a spot to take pleasant breaks. They wanted the parking lot to be more aesthetically pleasing and functional.

They wanted to make it easier for people to walk safely between the 2, 4, 6 trio and Building 20, the main administration building tucked into its own lushly landscaped corner across the drab parking lot and down a slope. Finally, the letter said, they wanted to "minimize the use of water as an architectural element." In other words, no big fancy fountains. The company would pay her $2,500 for creating and presenting her concepts.

In another office in another town, another landscape architect was receiving a similar letter. It would be a two-way competition. The winner would take away a handsome contract to do a landscape for one of the best-known companies in America at a site that thousands of employees and visitors would see every day. It was a competition worth winning.

The stark outline of the HP landscape site shows three buildings, three areas that could become landscaped entries, and an expansive parking lot. One landscape architect looks at the outline and envisions a central walkway, a Kelly-green lawn, clipped shrubs, tall pillars. Joni looks at the outline and sees three habitats, independent plant communities that form a progression from woodland to chaparral to grassland. She sees the natural settings she loves in the mountains, canyons, and meadows. And she notices an easily overlooked view of distant foothills that in their buff-colored summer skin look as soft and curvy as giant cat paws.

Certain elements pop out from the site for Joni. She knows

she wants three pathways with three habitats inspired by California's wildlands. She immediately begins to think of it thematically. She will call it Resurrecting Nature. She looks the word "resurrecting" up in the dictionary. It is too religious for her tastes, but she can't think of a more fitting word to describe the act of bringing life back to a place as lifeless as the asphalt plain.

Almost as soon as she has established the kernel of her ideas for the site, Joni begins to feel lost. Her creativity seems jammed in a state that won't take her ideas beyond the words in her mind. She can't see the ideas well enough to draw them or even express them coherently. One evening at home, she complains to Drew. She feels stuck, anxious, worried.

While Joni went through landscape-architecture training at Cal Poly, Drew finished his bachelor's degree in a major called "Law and Society" at U.C. Santa Barbara, about an hour's drive away. On weekends he drove up to Cal Poly and learned through Joni and her friends about the design process. At one point, he worked part-time in a landscape architect's office. His background has made Drew more than just a sympathetic sounding board.

"He has a sense of the professional quality that's necessary," Joni says. "And being a lawyer, he kind of puts that twist on it. If something is too abstract or too purple or too far in some particular direction, he'll say it, and that's good."

This time, Drew suggests Joni just start putting ideas on paper, even if only in words rather than drawings. She follows his advice, listing a few thoughts in a notebook she carries almost everywhere. Then, slowly, she begins sketching and a simple diagram of her ideas for HP unfolds. Joni begins to explain her thoughts and the diagram to her husband, looking for some clear thread to link the different habitats she wants to create with plants.

If you're talking about re-creating what may have been there, he tells her, incorporate the animals. Add elements that people find in a salmon habitat or cougar habitat or deer habitat, he urges. Maybe something as simple as a symbol of a cougar on a rock. Or maybe it would be a rock that people could sit on in a habitat that feels like one in which a cougar would live. Whatever the element, it would be linked to some animal and more clearly define each habitat, especially for people unfamiliar with the region's native plants. As Joni listens, she realizes Drew has found the missing link that will help her sell her landscape.

Later, at her office, she collects her small staff for a half day of brainstorming to refine the ideas and figure how best to represent them. The crew gathers around Joni's conference table and flips through magazines, looking for articles about wild animals and their habitats. Joni shares her rough diagrams, her ideas for different habitats, and together they create names for the pathways, names for the courtyards: Acorn Court, Deer Court, Cougar Den, Grizzly Flats, Salmon Run, Deer Path. They sketch rough line drawings on trace torn from one thinning roll. What if we did this? What about this, instead? The pencils race, the ideas fly. This is serious fun, this communal design session.

Designs by architects—either landscape or building—are often attributed to a single designer. A building designed by Robert A. M. Stern or Antoine Predock are Stern or Predock buildings. A landscape designed by George Hargreaves or Lawrence Halprin are Hargreaves or Halprin landscapes. But while lead designers get public credit for the work, more often than not the work is a collaboration. "It's never truly your own. It's sort of a composite," Joni explains. It is a combination of ideas from the lead architect and everyone else in the architect's firm who happens to share an opinion or put pen to paper—or cursor to computer screen—to help shape the design. Even in a one-person firm, the architect rarely works entirely alone. On virtually every project the client contributes ideas. In Joni's firm, where a lot of work must be completed by only a few people, nearly every project has every member's fingerprints on it.

On this project, Joni assigns Michael to do the graphic design and sketches that she will need for her presentation to Hewlett-Packard. Michael is new to the firm and only recently graduated from college. In most states, newly graduated landscape architects must work for about two years for a licensed landscape architect before they can take a licensing exam. Michael began working part-time for Joni only a few weeks earlier, to satisfy the apprenticeship requirement, and quickly became a full-timer. A shy, clean-cut surfer, he has always loved to draw and it is the drawing, as much as anything, that attracts him to landscape architecture. Joni hired him after seeing his portfolio; his style stood out for its clean discipline with sharp lines, angles, and details.

The HP design assignment is Michael's biggest project yet, but he manages to conceal any nervousness. As the brainstorming session ends, he collects the rough sketches and returns to his worktable in the big room. Then he begins to create new finer sketches and design plans.

For the next several days, Michael spends hours each workday hunched over his table, drawing. When the phone rings, sometimes with reluctance, sometimes with relief, he leaves to answer it. The phone is a minor irritant in the office. It is one of Joni's managerial headaches: whose time at the worktable is too valuable to leave to answer the phone? Judy answers it when she is in the office a few hours each week to do the bookkeeping and billing. The rest of the time, the three designers share the duty.

When the phone is quiet, Michael draws. It is a little intimidating at first. There is that empty page and he worries that what he does will look either too trite or too complex, that it won't get the right message across to the clients. Steady and quiet, he realizes he must trust himself and trust his intuition. There is comfort in knowing he can bounce ideas off of Joni and Robin. Through the week, Joni stops by his table occasionally to see how the work is progressing.

At first, Joni is worried that she isn't getting her ideas across to Michael. "Um, this is this deer thing," she later says with a laugh as she mocks her own approach to communicating. At times, Robin tries to help put into words the rush of ideas Joni wants to share with Michael. More often, Joni resorts to making little sketches on trace overlaid on Michael's drawings. "What do you think about doing something like this?" she'll ask. "Well, what about this?" he'll respond, wielding more trace and drawings. They draw and talk and continue to look at wilderness photos for inspiration.

Without knowing exactly how or when, the three designers begin to harmonize. Michael's final schematic and the sketches that accompany it capture what Joni wants, and then some. The day before Joni is scheduled to present the work at HP, Michael finishes all the drawings. Then the trio work late, bent over tables in the big room, listening to music and completing that simple and rewarding task: coloring it all with a rainbow of pencils.

VI

AS JONI JANECKI CONSIDERS THE OAK WOODland, chaparral, and meadow she wants to create at Hewlett-Packard, she is mixing garden design with plant ecology. She is thinking about communities, a very big concept in life sciences that, like the extended tendril of a grapevine, is gradually wending its way into the common vocabulary of landscape architecture.

Scientists define a community as the collection of living things that share a specific place or habitat. For example, a riverbank habitat and the plants, insects, and animals that live there make up a community. That includes everything from burrowing worms to ground-hugging salamanders to treetop-loving birds. When scientists talk about the nonliving things in that riverbank community, such as the water and soil, as well as the living things, they're talking about the ecosystem. Finally, when scientists ignore the animals and insects and look only at the plant life in the riverbank habitat—the cottonwoods and willows that shade the river from summer's hottest sun, the rushes and reeds that provide nesting grounds for ducks and frogs, the tiny wildflowers that add color to the green in spring—they are considering the plant community.

Nature is like a Jackson Pollock splash painting. It is a collection of hundreds of splotches, some different, some similar, some that flow together and at points become indistinct. Viewed from a distance, patterns jump out from the splotches, suggesting order in the apparent disorder. Whereas Pollock's splotches are made of paint, nature's splotches are made of plant communities. They repeat themselves, border each other, and often overlap, creating hybrid communities. Some plants appear in lots of different kinds of plant communities, some in only one. For example, lupine, a family of wildflowers whose blue, purple, and yellow spikes herald the approaching end of the rainy season in California, grow in airy grasslands as well as in crowded red-fir forests, among other places. In contrast, a West Coast version of the bug-eating pitcher plant, Darlingtonia californica, grows in the wild exclusively in mountain bogs.

It is impossible to say exactly how many different plant communities there are in the world. Scientists don't agree among themselves on the sort of system to use to identify a plant community. Do you identify it according to the dominant plants? Or do you identify it according to some physical characteristics of the area, such as soil conditions? Scholarly definitions have identified anywhere from a couple of dozen to more than two hundred different kinds of plant communities in California alone. Scientists love precision, and as they learn more, they find the subtle distinctions between areas that allow them to continue reclassifying communities. This precision helps them as they try to answer questions about how the earth evolved and how its natural systems work today.

For Joni, a landscape architect resurrecting nature on a parking lot in Palo Alto, precision becomes less important. The broad definitions of the region's plant communities will do as she tries to balance nature's realities with certain design principles. The end result she hopes to achieve will not be nature, or even a replica. It will be an interpretation that just through the plants she selects will come closer to the nature of the wild than most created landscapes in America. It will reflect the spirit of what was originally there, long before the first DeskJet printer rolled off a Hewlett-Packard assembly line. It will also echo the natural landscape still visible on the distant hills.

Designing with plant communities is fairly straightforward and simple: plant plants with the plants they live with in nature. Doing this has certain benefits for designers, according to the contemporary patriarch of plant-community design, landscape architect and University of Georgia professor Darrel Morrison. For starters, it simplifies plant selection. "When we learn plants by community, when we learn the ones that grow together in certain environments, it just makes designing with them so much more logical because you're not picking one from here and one from there and trying to put them together," Morrison says. "You're putting those together which occur together naturally." But, he adds, the landscape architect still has opportunities to incorporate design subtlety and complexity, the things that help make a created landscape comfortably ordered and interesting to people.

Another benefit Morrison attributes to plant-community design lies in the roadmap it provides designers to help them create landscapes that reflect the local environment and build upon a distinctive regional identity. It helps designers avoid any tendency to create cookie-cutter landscapes that have no sense of place. "I'm opposed to standardization," Morrison says, "and one of the most logical ways to [resist it] is to work with the unique vegetation of the region."

Typical suburban landscapes, with their mown lawns, clipped juniper, holly, or pittosporum hedges, and springtime borders of pansies, petunias, and impatiens, exemplify the kind of standardization that kills regional character. These landscapes are just "a collection of plants from all over, and oftentimes the same ones that are used everywhere else," Morrison laments. In contrast, landscapes designed with plant communities in mind draw from the palette of plants found together in local or regional wildlands. In suburban Phoenix, where 100-degree days are normal and desert cacti and succulents are the native plants, a plant-community landscape looks dramatically different from one in suburban Chicago, where prairie grasses once dominated. Nature didn't include the same plants in the same combinations in both locations.

The plant-community design concept makes it easier and, in some cases, more necessary to incorporate native plants into the human-made landscape. But it also begs the question: What is a native plant?

Fifty million years ago, tropical plants grew in a dense rain forest along coastal California. Botanists figure it looked like today's southern Mexico and Central America, thick with tree ferns and cycads. But as the climate cooled and dried, coastal California's plant communities evolved into coastal sage scrub, chaparral, oak woodland, and, farther north, evergreen forest.

Considering California's ancient plant history, is a tree fern now found only in southern Mexico also a California native? Most native-plant aficionados would say no. Usually they define a North American native plant as one that was growing here five hundred years ago, before European settlement. With European settlement, human impact on the continent's natural world and natural processes increased dramatically. The new settlers introduced hundreds of plants from Europe and elsewhere, some of which established themselves in the continent's wildlands.

Now, if a plant grew in a bog in New Jersey six hundred years ago, well before European settlement, and continues to grow there today, most people would consider it a native plant. But if a gardener in Wisconsin decided to plant that bog plant in his garden, would he be planting a native plant? By most definitions, the Wisconsin gardener would be planting an exotic plant that is native to North America but not to his state or region. Simply being native to one state or region does not make the plant native to all states, for purposes of native plant gardening.

Purists define a native plant as any plant that occurs naturally within a given place or ecosystem—such as a watershed or canyon or plateau. Among landscape architects, concern about such site-specific definition for a native plant becomes greatest during habitat-restoration projects. In rebuilding a wetland or woodland, landscape architects and ecologists strive to mimic what was once there to provide homes for the local—and native—wildlife and insects. In restoration, then, a native plant is typically defined as one that naturally occurred at that specific site.

Most native-plant advocates and landscape architects who use native plants in other types of created landscapes, such as gardens and urban parks, apply a broader geographic designation for native plants than the purists do. They usually define a native plant as one that occurs naturally within a state or region. This broader definition has a practical advantage: it opens up a bigger plant palette. Under this definition, an ironwood tree from Santa Cruz Island in California would not qualify as a native plant in Massachusetts any more than a New Zealand tea plant. But it would still qualify for inclusion in a native-plant landscape in, say, Montecito, even if it had never occurred there naturally. Joni's plans for neighboring savanna, woodland, and chaparral plantings at Hewlett-Packard would still qualify as a native-plant landscape under this definition.

Devoted gardeners who have a mild interest in native plants, and many mainstream nurseries, define native plants in continental terms. They define a native plant simply as one that grew naturally on the continent before Columbus arrived. State, regional, or ecosystem boundaries are mostly irrelevant in this definition. They feel perfectly comfortable calling a garden that includes different natives from Kansas, Washington State, and Florida a native-plant garden. It would be difficult for such a garden to echo or reflect the natural landscapes of any region. Indeed, it would probably be impossible to create a coherent plant-community design with such a mixed collection.

People who dismiss interest in native plants as just a marginal fanaticism—and there are many in the nursery industry who do—complain about the lack of one cohesive definition for native plant. Yet a common thread runs through all the definitions. That is that a native plant's origins can be traced back to a place in the United States where it still grows wild, where it is still a working member of a plant community. When wildlands diminish, this common thread weakens as more natives lose their original habitats and become living museum pieces in gardens. The Center for Plant Conservation, an organization made up of twenty-five arboreta and botanic gardens, estimates that about one-fourth of America's native plants need conservation and more than eight hundred are actually in danger of extinction. Loss of habitat is the primary threat to these plants. Even as people like Morrison and Joni consider ways to bring a plant's natural community into the created landscape, their constant worry is that the plant's original natural community is disappearing in the wild.

Hewlett-Packard added buildings to its headquarters as the company grew, and so the expansive site has been landscaped bit by bit. The result is an eclectic collection of plants that in some cases look skillfully arranged and in others haphazard. "It's kind of dated, with some modernized touches to it," Joni observes. "There's no sense of identity anywhere. There are no exclamantion points: this is here, this is the place, this is something special. It's all kind of the same."

Nevertheless, there is surprising variety among the plants. As Phil Koenig tools around the HP grounds in his golf cart, he points out random plantings of California natives. There are manzanitas, red-barked shrubs found throughout the state's wildlands. There are ceanothus, the flowering wild lilac shrubs that in spring brighten the state's chaparral and woodlands with explosions of blue, lavender, or white flowers. A few coast redwoods grow in a group, Monterey pines shade cars in a parking lot. In various spots around the property—in front of buildings, along the street, beneath a small grove of trees—Koenig has struggled with native bunch grasses, refugees from California's vanishing grasslands.

These plantings are mixed among the big-rooted carob trees, flowering pear trees, cotoneaster bushes, turf grass, and dozens of other exotics. Neither the exotics nor the natives are without problems, according to Koenig. "See those magnolia trees? Those carob trees?" He points to several whose roots, working like heavy iron crowbars, have buckled the asphalt. "They really have to go." Referring to a collection of wide-shouldered pines, he says, "These Monterey pines are not a desirable tree really, and they've been banged up pretty bad. They've got pitch moth and other things, so they'll probably go."

The native bunch grasses have been a significant headache for Koenig. Unlike turf grass, which is trimmed short regularly, bunch grasses are meant to grow long. Some respond to California's rain-free summers by going dormant, turning from green to tan. Planted in a mass, bunch grass looks like an undulating wave of flexible fiber when a light breeze blows over. But to someone unfamiliar with it, bunch grass looks like turf gone wild, a lawn in need of a mower and a long drink of water.

Phil pulls the cart up to the edge of a recently planted tiny meadow of four kinds of native grasses. "People aren't accepting of it. They want to see it mowed," he says, sighing. Along a street-side strip on the edge of the HP complex, he has planted a swath of bunch grass called red fescue and he has heard complaints. "People think we're not doing our maintenance," he explains. They can't tolerate grasses that can look like tawny living versions of a toy troll's wild haircut. For such folks, green is the only acceptable grass color and military haircut short is the only tolerable length. Part of the challenge for Phil and the landscape maintenance crew is learning how to care for the bunch grass in a way that makes it look maintained without destroying its naturally shaggy characteristics. Cutting it away from the edge, cutting it away from the rocks is one way to do this, Phil says. Meanwhile, he considers replacing the red fescue with other grasses that wear their blades more conservatively. It might ease some of the complaints.

Joni sympathizes with Phil's grass problems. She is particularly fond of native grasses and has even served as an officer in the California Native Grass Association. But she has heard the complaints, too, about the grasses and native plants in general. "They're just a bunch of weeds," she has heard detractors say. As she prepares to present her firm's concepts for the new landscape, she knows she may encounter similar resistence from HP. She will have to persuade them that her basic ideas are right for the site, that her team is the best one for the job, and hope that talks don't get bogged down in plant politics.

On presentation day, Joni arrives at HP loaded down with a heavy satchel and two large foam-core boards plastered with colored plans and sketches. The lone receptionist in the simply decorated lobby issues Joni a form that becomes a hall pass. Then one of the selection team arrives and leads Joni into the heart of the building. They walk along a hallway, down stairs, past huge rooms of partitioned work areas—an HP standard for workplace design—and finally into a functionally furnished conference area where the rest of the five-member selection team waits. She greets everyone, arranges the boards, and hands out photocopied sketches of the main ideas. Then she launches into her presentation.

Had she known landscape architects have to spend so much time speaking in front of groups, she later says, she might never have entered the profession. She isn't thrilled about public speaking—in college, it would literally make her sick—but she has learned to do it well, and as she runs through her plans for HP, she is confident and at ease.

Joni explains that she will use habitats as design models for the HP landscape. She describes the courtyards—Grizzly Flats, Acorn Court, Deer Court, Cougar Den—and pathways—Salmon Run, Deer Path, Cougar Corridor. The three paths will cross the parking lot and link the trio of buildings to the main administration building, giving employees safe and easy routes to follow. She recommends adding greenery to the parking lot to break up the asphalt and make it more appealing to those looking down from upper floors. Part of the lot will have chaparral plantings, part savanna plantings to be consistent with the linking courtyards. She talks about technical elements that will save water and money. There will be catch basins to collect rainwater and direct it to the adjacent water-recycling facility.

Each member of the selection team holds an evaluation sheet, and after Joni leaves, they rank her ideas for such things as cost and design. Later, they will compare her rankings to those they give the other firm competing for the job. The ranking system ensures that no single voice on the selection team dominates.

One selection-team member later describes the competing plan—from a well-known San Francisco firm—as "a typical corporate landscape that we see all over." It includes a central walkway, turf, and pillars, and suggests an approach that deviates from the low-key, unpretentious image that has become known as part of the "HP Way."

Weeks later, Joni has trouble keeping a straight face when discussing the animal names her firm attached to its plan's courtyards and paths. They are campy and cute, she realizes, but they do the job. They convey the message that each area will be linked to some specific natural setting. The message and the concepts "kind of blew our socks off," Phil recalls weeks after the presentation. "She went beyond our initial expectation. It was something that was very functional. She addressed every single problem that we wanted addressed."

For Shokrai, the plan was almost mesmerizing. "She had

names for every area. It was like a storybook for me." It was also something that Shokrai, who has a college-age son, felt would appeal to a younger generation which is more environmentally conscious and which comprises the future workforce. It also appealed to his own feelings about nature and how it should be expressed. "I don't like most landscaping because everything is so straight. The plants are cut straight and I don't like that."

The rest of the team agreed. When scores were tallied, their choice was clear. Joni won the job.

In Montecito, Abbe and Dennis Sands celebrated their son's birthday with a party in their relatively bare yard. It was a Pog party for fourteen active seven-year-olds. There were water-balloon fights and silly string squirtings, lots of running and dodging. Nobody had to worry about damaging some delicate perennial bed or manicured lawn as they raced after each other. There was freedom in this yard of dirt and trees.

To decorate beforehand, the Sands threw brightly colored rolls of paper streamers into the oak tree and watched them unravel among the branches. Then they all stood back and admired the look. "It was the first time there was color anywhere," Abbe says later. "Everything had been brown and green and dirt. Even the kids said, 'This looks pretty.' It showed that this could really look beautiful if we had something other than the browns and the dirt. That was funny. It felt decorated for a minute."

It made the family that much more anxious to see some landscaping. So when a Federal Express truck pulled up one sunny Thursday and dropped off a mailing tube, Abbe took it into the house, tore it open, and eagerly unrolled Joni's design plans. Dennis was in Los Angeles for a few days working on a project. Her son was at her elbow, squirming for a view. Abbe loved what she saw. "I had certain things that I thought it would be, and it was different and better."

But she was worried, too. The landscape the plan proposed looked impossibly expensive. "That was the part of it that was almost scary," she recalls. "Then I thought I couldn't wait for Dennis to see it, but I didn't want to influence him by saying to him on the phone, 'We can't afford it! We can't do any of it.' "

Abbe reminded herself that when she first received Joni's plans for their other home, she felt the same combination of delight and trepidation. "Then I started to dissect it a little bit, sort of squinted my eyes and said, 'Okay, if we just do the hardscape and get the form going, then everything else could follow. What could we eliminate? If this is the extreme, what could be a simpler task to undertake?' And then, as you start looking, you go, 'Well, no, it's not so bad. If we use this stone instead of this stone or this material instead of that and don't get into the planting stage so fast, then we probably could do this in our lifetime.' "

She called in Larry Hochhalter, a craftsman who was doing some work on the house. What did he think, she asked. It looked good to Larry, and he started giving rough estimates on costs. "It became even more frightening," Abbe recalls.

She telephoned Dennis and arranged to show him the plans in Los Angeles over the weekend. She didn't reveal much, just that "it's pretty overwhelming and Joni put the monkey tree in a very interesting spot."

Abbe worried that Dennis wouldn't like the placement of the monkey puzzle outside his office window. Maybe he wanted it to be more of a focal point, the centerpiece of the landscape. But her concern was unwarranted. He didn't have any qualms about the design. The elements that Joni had liked the most by the time she finished the plan were the ones that the Sands liked as well.

"What she did was make all the areas of the house important and very beautiful, so you don't have a sense of front yard, back yard. The whole thing works so nicely. And the way she put the driveway in, it just keeps it part of the landscaping instead of a whole separate motor area, which it is now," Abbe explains. "And then to walk up to the front of the house instead of driving up to the front of the house makes it very special, too. It gives it a real garden flow. With the arbor at the entry, the experience becomes entering the garden, you know, and entering this setting that is so inviting. The meadow—she said she wants to put some wildflowers in the meadow—and I just loved that she called this little grassy area the meadow. It's so cute."

A week later, the Sands celebrated Thanksgiving with relatives in their new home. They showed off the plans, and everyone approved. Putting in the landscape still looked expensive to Dennis and Abbe, but as they listened to their children and their relatives rave about the design, getting it built seemed more possible. They would do the landscaping as they had remodeled the house, bit by bit, section by section, project by project. This was just the beginning. They decided to ask Joni to put together a cost estimate with a phasing plan, suggesting which parts should be done first, second, and so on. Later, they could ask her to do lighting plans, irrigation plans, and a planting plan, they figured. Then they would get to work.

Joni was on a roll.

VII

IT IS PRESIDENTS DAY, AND ROBIN MACLEAN IS ON duty for Janecki and Associates. A small company facing a suddenly heavy workload has little time for national holidays. Robin's consolation comes in knowing that at least part of her day's work will be outdoors and away from her desk.

By 9 a.m., she is on the road, steering her fading red, canvas-topped jeep past acres of artichokes. The motor's rumble and the wind rattling through small openings in the jeep's plastic zippered windows make normal conversation impossible. So she talks loud as she points out the sights. The artichokes grow in tight rows, looking like large leafy dusters with topknots of green fruit. Judy and Joni call the plants "chemchokes," Robin yells above the motor. The name is a not-so-subtle commentary on this edible plant's apparent reliance on pesticides to become a valuable farm crop. Robin notes that the organic variety tends to host a worm or two, an unpleasant discovery that prompts her to abandon pesticide-avoidance when she craves an artichoke.

These farmlands lie on the edge of downtown Castroville, artichoke capital of the world. It is a dusty town south of Santa Cruz, on the road to Salinas, today's destination. This is the country John Steinbeck wrote about, where farming's romance is dulled by harsh realities. These fields are only freeway minutes from so hip Santa Cruz and très chic Carmel, but the towns seem decades apart. An increase of people and houses since Steinbeck's time hasn't obliterated this area's backbreaking vegetable farming, and the stark contrast between the people who work the fields and the people who don't.

The fields continue, though the crops change to lettuce and strawberries, as the jeep moves closer to an interior freeway and then into Salinas. The farmlands disappear, giving way to new shopping centers and fast-food outlets. Then fields appear again, this time freshly plowed and waiting for planting. Across the street from the fields stands a hulking tract of new homes, mostly two-story numbers painted in shades of beige. The houses continue on one side and the fields on another for several blocks. Then the houses stop and the road dead-ends where a slope and a creek bed begin. It is Natividad Creek, the namesake of the still incomplete new park it runs through.

Robin stops the jeep and saunters toward a sloped bank, scanning the landscape along the way. Hay bales huddle like temporary dams along sections of the silty creek bed. They edge a sandy island to protect it from eroding when the seasonal creek flows hard after winter rains. Willows are thick on the island and along the creek's opposite, flatter bank.

Nothing grows on the bank where Robin now stands. A

light grayish green substance that looks like paint covers it. Robin stoops and prods the substance with her fingers. "It's rock-hard," she grumbles.

The substance is a mixture of fertilizer, water, a papery mulch, and wildflower seeds. This bank has been hydroseeded. Just a week ago, workers using hoses attached to tanks filled with the mixture sprayed it on the bank. Hydroseeding is a fast method to spread seed and keep it fertilized and in one place until it roots. The problem here is that the contractor responsible for the seeding has been running behind schedule on the park's construction. The seeds should have been spread many weeks earlier, as the rainy season was beginning. Instead, the seeds were spread late in the season, and a week without moisture has hardened the seed-and-mulch mixture. Now Robin worries that the seeds won't get enough rain to break through the cement-like surface.

The late seeding is one of many slowdowns facing this project. The contractor still has not placed matting along another part of the creek to prevent erosion. In some cases, the landscape architect would be responsible for recommending a contractor and then making sure the contractor meets schedules. This is a city-led project, though, so the contractor was selected through a bidding process and reports directly to the city's staff. Janecki and Associates have no say in the hydroseeding or the matting at this point. Robin makes a note of it anyway, in case the plants don't grow or the slope erodes.

Robin turns her attention away from the hydroseed and eases down the slope for a closer look at the hay bales. The bales anchor young willows that reach up from them like leafy sticks. Willows are among the workhorse plants of riparian habitats, the term scientists use to describe a riverbank community. There are thirty-one willow species in California alone, adapted to different elevations and climates, but always planted near water. Their strong roots play havoc with city sidewalks but are saviors to creek banks and sandbars that need help staying in place. Willows also grow quickly. In five years or so, the ones in the hay bales will be as large as the mature trees on the creek's banks.

The young willows look spindly but healthy. Satisfied with their progress, Robin hikes back up the slope to her jeep, a vehicle that has reliably carried her on three journeys across the United States. On the latest journey, it brought her out here after five years of work at the Boston office of a huge environmental consulting firm whose services include landscape architecture. It was the kind of place that had hundreds of employees in offices around the world. At the firm's Boston office, computers with the latest software were abundant. Robin learned to use them to create base maps, construction drawings, and even some design work. For that reason, among others, she greatly values her post-grad time in Boston. Generally, though, she hated working for a large corporation. When she finally quit, she didn't know where she would work again, but knew she wanted to be in a smaller office.

Timing worked in Robin's favor. Her return trip to California coincided with her college friend Joni's start-up of Janecki and Associates. Joni's one-woman business was taking off and she needed help. The two women struck a deal while hiking in the hills around Santa Cruz. Robin would join Joni as an employee, not a partner, for as long as the work lasted. Now, two years later, the work seems to be flowing their way like a stream at spring thaw. Indeed, Robin muses, the challenge for Joni and the firm in the next year is going to be deciding how much work to take and how big the firm should get.

Robin drives half a block back along the farm fields, turns onto a residential road that carries her half the length of the park-to-be, then up another road that cuts the park in two. She pulls onto a street that winds along the upper side of the park and brings her jeep to a stop at the curb. Modest single-story tract homes sit across the street from a wide strip of unplanted dirt that quickly falls off into a hundred-yard slope which ends where the park's flatland begins.

The park rests on a floodplain, bordered on its length by rising slopes that flatten into housing tracts. Running through it and beyond is Natividad Creek. On paper, the park-to-be has been roughly divided into two halves. One half includes the portion Robin has just inspected, where part of the creek remains substantially wild and its surrounding brush and trees are main features. The other half lies on this slope and the flat below. Here human engineering has bound parts of the creek in concrete or routinely compacted its clayey banks, converting it over the years to a barren ditch designed to do little else but carry rainwater to the ocean without disturbing homes. These days the creek looks even more barren than usual because the land surrounding it has been scraped clean and moved about by heavy tractors shaping what will become parking lots, picnic areas, pathways, and tennis courts. Soon this will be a place where people will be encouraged to play, in contrast to the other end of the park, where restoring the natural world takes precedence.

The Janecki firm was hired to come up with a planting plan to mimic nature on the creek's banks, including the wilder stretch at the quiet end of the park. It has also been asked to create a planting plan for the hillsides and flats around the playing courts and parking lots on the active part of the park. All together, the firm is responsible for designing the planting scheme for about one-fourth of the park's sixty-four acres.

Robin hops out of her jeep and changes from fashionable shiny black-laced shoes into a pair of hiking boots. Tricia Lowe, a marine-biology graduate student interested in habitat restoration, arrives in an old red Volkswagen Rabbit. Tricia, a trim brunette, is running late today and swiftly unloads a bundle of thin, yard-long bamboo sticks and several rolls of colored plastic ribbon. On the three-acre slope below the two women, beribboned sticks already stand at attention. The sun is shining on this mid-February morning, and only occasionally a breeze gathers enough strength to chill the air, so Robin decides to leave her pullover in the jeep before she walks over to greet Tricia.

This is a stakeout. Tricia has spent a portion of the last several days reviewing the firm's planting plan for the park and positioning the sticks to mark where each plant will be placed on the slope. She works part-time for Return of the Natives, a local nonprofit organization dedicated to teaching children about the environment and about science through native plants, including introducing native plants to the created landscape.

In the last decade, organizations have sprung up in Great Britain, Canada, and the United States that emphasize returning native plants and natural-looking landscapes to schoolyards. In Canada, one national program run by the Evergreen Foundation has involved more than a thousand schools in a school-grounds naturalization program. In the United States, similar efforts tend to be conducted by local or regional groups and are harder to track, but there are at least twenty organizations that, like Return of the Natives, work to some degree to bring native plants and natural landscapes into this country's schoolyards and curricula, replacing the standard schoolyard landscape of asphalt, dirt, lawn, and clipped banks of indistinct shrubs and trees.

That typical schoolyard landscape offers nothing from a nature-study standpoint, says Bruce Stewart, an environmental educator and one of the Return of the Natives founders. The shrubs and trees aren't selected for their ability to attract butterflies or feed birds native to the area. The lawn consists of only one or two types of grass and is regularly clipped short, providing no food or cover for anything, even as it drains maintenance dollars because of its constant need for mowing and fertilizing. In contrast, Stewart says, a schoolground landscaped with a variety of native plants introduces biological diversity. The landscape attracts native insects and birds. It also becomes a lively tool for teaching children about wildlands and the ecosystem.

Teachers and school principals in Salinas were enthusiastic about the native landscape idea, and with a handful of people that included a Moss Landing Marine Laboratories ecologist, an environmental educator, and Joni Janecki, formed

Return of the Natives. Within months, the group was holding workshops to train schoolteachers to grow native plants and use them to teach. The group also established small greenhouses at several schools for native plant propagation, and Joni helped draft schoolyard landscape plans for one particularly enthusiastic group of teachers.

Most significant, the city of Salinas prodded the group to look beyond schoolyards by contracting it to help plant part of the Natividad Creek Park landscape Joni's firm has designed. So now Tricia is racing to finish organizational details, from placing stakes to fetching plants to collecting tools, before the park's first planting begins. In less than forty-eight hours, busloads of students will arrive—a shovel-bearing labor force. Today this steep slope is mostly covered with a weedy mixture of unwanted grass. If everything goes according to plan, by Wednesday evening the weeds will be replaced by native shrubs, trees, and grasses.

Robin has come here to review the stake placement and answer last-minute questions. Tricia leads Robin to a spot on the slope where she has already set bamboo markers, each bearing a colored ribbon coded to indicate a specific type of plant. The landscape architect scans their arrangement. The colored ribbons barely move in the breeze.

"Massing is the key word," Robin says as she considers the sticks planted among the weeds.

"What's that?" Tricia asks.

"Massing is the key word. You can do almost anything if you mass it."

"Clumping? You mean into groups of three and five?"

"Yeah," Robin confirms. "Then it can't go wrong." A

plant left standing alone looks lonely. A group looks comfortable.

The plant list for this spot reads like a who's who of the best-known California natives. There will be bush monkey flower, admirable for its light-apricot-colored flowers. There will be California sagebrush, feathery green in winter and spring, soft brown and gray during the dry summer. Fragrant black sage, colorful lupine, buckeyes with their giant seeds which look like oversized chestnuts, several bunch grasses, and young oaks. Manzanita. Coffeeberry. Coyote bush. California fuchsia. Toyon. The list goes on.

"This is probably one of the tightest clusters," Tricia says, pointing to a group of three sticks spaced about eighteen inches apart. "Is it too tight?"

"No, I don't think so," Robin says. As she continues walking, she suggests moving a few markers this way or that. The women discuss which nurseries will be delivering plants and which will require pickup before Wednesday morning. Tricia confides that her main worry is that, before planting day, off-road vehicle riders will decide the stakes make a great obstacle course. Fears of vandalism have hovered over this park since before the first earthmover arrived. So far, though, the project has been left untouched.

Robin ends the consultation convinced that the hillside plan is under control. She climbs back into her rugged vehicle for the ride back to the office. Tricia remains behind, balanced on the slope, shin-deep in weeds, pushing thin bamboo into the ground.

From the road, as Robin drives away, the park looks more like a flat-bottomed valley of nude flats and weedy hillsides than like a place that will draw people and harbor wildlife. It takes an imaginative mind to see what it will become. Robin thrives on this park-creating process, watching a plot of tractor-scarred land evolve into an oasis of play courts and lush landscape. "The park has been wonderful," she yells above the jeep engine. "It's like watching a child grow."

Parks in America have had several heydays. The first was during the last half of the nineteenth century, when a reform-minded elite, including Olmsted, Sr., decided that city parks were essential to civic health. Parks, these reformers said, were a social equalizer where wealthy and poor could enjoy the same pleasures—fresh air, pleasant surroundings, healthful sports, and just plain people-watching.

Parks were a family therapist without the hourly fees, a fitness club without the monthly membership, and a live theater without the ticket prices. Park construction, not incidentally, also provided a great opportunity to design an important landscape on a grand scale that could touch lives. As Olmsted noted in an architect's report in 1867, "When entirely freed from extraneous considerations the central idea of a large public park is manifestly that of a work of art, of a peculiar character undoubtedly, but nevertheless designed at the outset as all other works of art are designed, with the intention of producing, through the exercise of the natural perceptions, a certain effect upon the mind and the character of those who approach it."

More recently, parks had a boom period during the massive development and economic growth that followed World

War II. Many cities, counties, and states had generous and growing budgets that they shared with their parks departments. Walt Tryon, a landscape architect and professor at Cal Poly San Luis Obispo, recalls working simultaneously on designs for three new regional parks in two Maryland counties in the late 1960s. One of the counties, Prince Georges, was one of the fastest growing in America at the time. Money was pouring into the region and the population growth accompanied intense pressure to preserve open space.

Work on the parks had to be done so quickly that Tryon designed and drafted at a table in a converted school bus that could be moved from one park site to the next. He had to be close to the action, available to make a decision or a change in a plan at a moment's notice. "A master plan would be approved—we would make presentations to the park commissioners—and as soon as the approval came in, they immediately started construction," Tryon recalls of that golden park-building age.

Today is not a heydey for parks. American towns and cities are struggling to meet expenses for crime-fighting and the infrastructure that holds a city together—water, sewers, roads, firefighters. Their leaders complain they have little if anything left for park construction. Salinas faces the same budget-balancing challenges as most cities. But it has become a bedroom community for commuters to white-collar jobs in other areas, especially the technology-intensive Silicon Valley. New houses and schools have replaced acres of farmland on the north end of town. This housing development mini-boom and the corresponding developer fees have helped feed a modest piggy bank for park construction.

More than two decades ago, Ed Piper abandoned a brief

career as a landscape architect because he found too much of the work tedious. He traded in life at the drafting table for a planning-related job with the city of Salinas. Now responsible for getting a rare new park built, he finds himself gleefully swept up in landscape planning.

A ruggedly handsome man, Piper blocked out spots for the picnic tables, parking lots, basketball courts, playgrounds, amphitheater, and other recreational amenities for Natividad Creek Park. He figured what portion of the park would be left to nature, what portion reserved for recreation. Then, as he was considering how to make the most of the park's limited budget, Piper's park evolved into a peculiar combination of educational tool and community-building program. What might have been a typical top-down process changed course when, at an early Return of the Natives meeting, he suggested the group help plant the park.

In fact, the park had to be different to exist at all. For one thing, the city was obligated under an agreement with the state to restore three acres of Natividad Creek to its long-ago wild condition. For another, even with the developer fees set aside, there wasn't enough money available from city coffers to build all the things people wanted in the park. It would take creative thinking to squeeze enough from the budget to pay for construction. Finally, the Natividad Creek's neighbors worried about park crime even before the first construction crew arrived. Experience suggested that simply relying on police to respond at the first sign of suspicious activity wasn't going to be enough to prevent park vandalism and keep criminals out.

Piper and the Return of the Natives founders believed that,

with the help of some city money and state grants, Return of the Natives could grow and plant native plants in the Natividad Creek Park. The students would learn how plants grow and actually have a planting experience. The city would get more landscaping at less cost than a regular landscape-contractor or city-maintenance crew could provide. The park and its creek-bed restoration would become an educational tool, a living laboratory for students at every level, but especially for older students interested in seeing how a damaged creek could be brought back to life. It would be the first step toward restoring a many-fingered watershed crisscrossing the local valleys and leading to Monterey Bay. Finally, by involving schoolchildren and the community in the planting, Piper hoped that Return of the Natives and the city staff would help create a broad-based feeling of park stewardship. That feeling, he hoped, would help control the crime and vandalism that so worried the neighbors.

As Robin winds her way back through farm fields toward the coast, the air takes on a salty crispness. The sky is clear and it would be a good day to drive the back roads toward the redwood forests that hug the hills just east of Santa Cruz. But work calls. She decides a pleasant compromise between the lure of outdoor leisure and the demands of indoor labor would be a brief detour to a wholesale nursery.

Robin turns off the coastal highway at a nearly invisible dirt road and follows it up a rise. The road bisects fallow fields overgrown with weeds. After three minutes of dusty driving, she sees a bland-looking stucco house ahead. The road narrows into a driveway that passes to the rear of the house. A few yards from the house sit weathered wooden sheds and a greenhouse. Two friendly shepherd dogs, all tongues and tails, greet the jeep. After she parks, Robin pauses for a moment to take in the view that stretches beyond and below this mesa. Winding azure waters of Elkhorn Slough, backed by green hills resembling a brocade of tree canopies, scrub and grasses, command attention.

She strolls toward the sheds and in the shade of a thin screen roof she finds two young men at work. One sits on an overturned bucket, pulling small weeds from plugs of native grass growing in six-inch-long yellow tubes called stubbies. They don't use pesticides here and much of the staff's time is spent weeding. Nearby, eight-packs of ten-inch-long pots, called deepots, hold baby trees that look like little more than bare upright branches. More deepots and stubbies and larger gallon pots bearing plants sit in neat rows under the screen and beside the greenhouse.

This is Elkhorn Ranch, a place and a nursery that share the same name. The place is 1,200 acres of former pasture and farmland purchased in 1987 by the late David Packard, a founder of Hewlett-Packard and nearly omnipresent in this part of the state. An avid sportsman and conservationist, Packard bought this land planning to restore its oak woodlands and freshwater habitat at the edge of the slough, to increase the feeding and resting space for ducks and migratory birds. The plant nursery was first established to collect and grow native plants for the ranch restoration projects. But as the work progressed, Paul Kephart, the nursery's founding manager, urged that the nursery's mission be expanded to grow native plants to sell to others. Packard agreed, but with one condition: The nursery had to be self-sufficient, at least break even each year.

Within just a few years, the nursery was growing about 275 different species of native plants. It also had become one of a handful of prime sources in the state for native grass seed. Its small staff grows close to a hundred acres of different kinds of native grass, bagging the seed for sale. They bundle the grass straw into bales to be sold as a mulch that smothers weeds and prevents the wind from blowing the soil away.

Kephart, a tall, husky man with a thick sweep of blond hair combed back from his forehead, was once a painter of Western art. Now he is dedicated to the self-taught trades of nurseryman, landscape designer, and restorationist. "I'm kind of a rogue naturalist," he says.

He has watched as a mini-explosion in the restoration of natural areas, on public and private property, has occurred in the region. Hand in hand with that, he has seen the demand for native plants escalate and is anxious to expand and modernize this modest nursery. Not counting the fields of native grasses, the actual nursery takes up only a few acres, most of it enclosed in rough-hewn sheds, arbor, and greenhouse. "I call it the Flintstone Nursery," Kephart jokes. "We probably have the most basic facility that anyone has ever used for growing plants."

If there is a typical native-plant wholesale nursery, it is one that covers only a few acres, compared to the larger spreads of mainstream all-purpose wholesale nurseries, many of which cover dozens of acres or more. A high proportion of native-plant nurseries seem to have been started since the early 1970s by people whose interest in plants was shaped by a concern for the environment.

Elkhorn Ranch Nursery, like many specialty and mainstream wholesale nurseries, grows a lot of its plants on contract. Landscape architects and others who need truckloads of plants for a project go to Elkhorn Ranch and put in an order as soon as they know their plant list. The Elkhorn staff will then grow what's on the list. Since few commercial nurseries carry large quantities or varieties of native plants, a contract nursery that specializes in natives is like an oasis in a desert for a landscape architecture firm like Joni's. But it takes some planning to use it right. Wait too late to place an order and the plants won't be ready on time. If a project is delayed, an order of four-inch-pot plants can become gallon plants by the time they leave the nursery.

Elkhorn Ranch is among a handful of nurseries that provide plants for Natividad Creek Park. Robin examines some of the grasses growing in the yellow stubbies. They look like thatches of fine green hair. She absently runs her hands through the soft, flexible blades. She asks one of the young men if the plants for the park are going to be ready as scheduled. He assures her they will be; the young grasses in the stubbies are destined for the park.

A quarter-acre field next to the greenhouse has been planted with flowering perennials. Before Robin leaves the nursery to return to work, she strolls among the young plants, identifying the ones she knows, admiring the ones she doesn't. She comes to the end of the field and again takes in the view of the slough. Native plants grow on its banks and islands, and oaks grow on the rolling hills nearby. Somewhere in that natural landscape, plants like the ones in the field at this nursery grow wild. From this mesa, the distant landscape looks idyllic. It looks the way all this region once looked, before settlers and bulldozers and construction crews came. It is a look Robin hopes to see reflected one day at Natividad Creek Park.

VIII

ED PIPER LEANS AGAINST HIS TOYOTA 4RUNNER truck and looks out over the barren, unfinished park that drops off from this mesa. All around him, low-key chaos reigns. In thirty minutes, the first children will arrive to help plant. Tricia Lowe and a platoon of adult volunteers scurry around just yards away, arranging tools, carrying potted shrubs to designated spots on the steep slope, reviewing logistics. Ed wears a bemused expression as he alternately watches the activity and stares out at his grand project.

He always wanted Natividad Creek Park to be different from other Salinas parks. He wanted it to be more wildland natural than parks landscaped in formal designs with ornamental shrubs from around the world. He wanted the new park to provide a well-defined sense of place. He wanted it to say "This is California," the way coast live oak and russet-barked manzanita do. He wanted people to connect with the wildlands visible in the distance, to understand those wildlands.

"We're looking to try to re-create an environment that once existed here, so that the people living in the community, the children in the community, can learn about it," he explains as a small pickup truck delivering pots of native shrubs stops at the curb. But environmental education is only one reason Ed became convinced that planting natives would be a good idea. He also wanted to minimize the park's landscape maintenance costs, and he needed to keep water demand low.

Reducing water bills is one of the most common reasons people in almost every part of the country give for turning to native plants. The minute a drought breaks out—and they seem to be breaking out with increasing frequency—so does interest in plants that tolerate long, dry summers. When gardeners cry for help during droughts, native plants pop up in garden stores like mushrooms in damp forest duff. Shelves that only weeks earlier carried truckloads of thirsty delicacies suddenly carry natives long adapted to periodic dry spells. Plants that hikers recognize replace plants so highly bred that they have no direct link to any natural habitat. Then, when the drought subsides, mainstream garden centers shrink their native-plant stock to only a few common natives or take it out entirely.

That here-today, gone-tomorrow attitude drives native plant enthusiasts nuts. So do the myths that cause setbacks whenever general interest in native plants surges. One is that all native plants are drought-tolerant. True, many native plants don't need a lot of water, having adapted to climate cycles that include dry seasons. In the Southwest, for instance, some natives automatically go into dormancy in the summer—their growth stops and their metabolism slows down. Water these plants during the summer months and you risk killing them. Transplant them to the Midwest, where summers are humid and rainy, and they drop dead. Their roots rot away.

But a lot of other natives grow in wet habitats and *do* need water, even during dry years and dry seasons. If you plant one of these in a sunny, dry place, its leaves burn, its roots wither, and it dies. A fern from an Oregon forest is not going to be happy in the Arizona desert. In short, native plants share something with even the most overused exotic: they will thrive only in the right place and with the right care.

Another myth about native plants is that they don't require maintenance. Often, the best care for native plants *is* little care. Property owners and gardeners, especially reluctant gardeners, warm to this promise like mosquitoes to a bare shoulder. However, *little* care doesn't mean *no* care. "Too many times a native garden is put in and people hate it because it looks wild and leggy like a weed patch," Robin MacLean says. "But it's only because the plants haven't been maintained. Or they're not weeded properly, or they're pruned wrong."

Like any plant sold in a garden center, native plants need certain soil types, soil nutrients, and watering regimens. Generally, a native plant that is planted in native soil (not the second or third layer down after topsoil has been scraped away during grading) doesn't need special fertilizers. Its species has adapted to the local soil's composition. To thrive, it may need nothing more than occasional water to supplement seasonal rains. If it is a perennial, it might need to be cut back every year or two, just like a lot of exotic perennials, to satisfy a gardener's version of worthiness. A well-planned native-plant landscape rarely requires pesticides. In fact, using pesticides is almost antithetical to the natural atmosphere that leads many native-plant gardeners to opt for natives.

The key to an attractive, low-maintenance native-plant landscape is to make sure the landscape is designed with local climate and soil conditions in mind. That is why Ed Piper brought Joni Janecki and her firm in to create the Natividad Creek Park's planting plan. "I'm a designer," he says. "I'm not an expert in native plants."

There was one more reason Ed wanted to use native plants. In fact, in this one thing, he had no choice. He had to satisfy a state requirement that the city restore the wild end of the creek, and proper restoration means using native plants.

Restoration, especially of wetland habitats like Natividad Creek, has become hot stuff in this country since the early 1980s. Community members sometimes decide to take on the job of cleaning up a river or replanting a scarred hillside themselves. But, more typically, restoration begins with a government agency prodding itself, a public institution, or a private developer into fixing a place, often as payoff for damage done somewhere else.

Natural systems, from a pine forest to a creek-side habitat, are complex. They involve soil and its mineral composition, water and the way it moves, plants and what they need and who they feed, insects and what they pollinate, animals and how they survive. Even one system is more than one person alone can understand in detail. Restoration is usually a group effort, and the people involved constantly refine how best to do it, even as they plan and plant. As one active restorationist explains, restoration is not a single science "but a cooperative effort—a way of applying science, engineering, and design."

Landscape architects, with backgrounds that make them both experts and utility players, are often part of a restoration team. On Natividad Creek, Joni has come up with a planting scheme that will jump-start the creek side's return to what it was before people started tearing it up. The damage was done by everything from bulldozers that moved through the creek bed as they graded nearby streets and housing tracts to anonymous trashhounds who pegged this spot as a free dumpsite for old tires, broken concrete, and stolen bicycles.

Not many years ago, restoring or reclaiming a damaged natural area didn't necessarily include native plants. Restorationists would turn to just about any plant that would thrive, thinking less about the ecosystem or systematic restoration. Miles of coastal beach dunes—where people planted South African ice plant and European beach grasses to stabilize the sand, driving out native dune plants as they did so—are ample evidence of this thinking. In recent years, as researchers have refined their understanding of natural systems, they have turned almost exclusively to native plants in restoration. Current efforts often involve tearing out the exotic plant remnants of past restorations.

One of the main goals of restoration is to return an ecosystem to health. Knowing how to do this, though, requires determining its level of health or sickness. In an ideal world, says botanist Al Flinck, to measure ecosystem health a scientist or team would count and categorize all the system's living things, and evaluate their number and condition. But such counting, measuring, and categorizing is usually not practical. A lot of living organisms move around constantly and are difficult to see or catch. Even counting and evaluating everything in just one small area would take years, Flinck notes, which wouldn't be soon enough for many places. "These natural ecosystems are disappearing at a rate faster than we can understand them."

For a quicker, more practical measure of relative health, scientists have turned to an ecosystem's plant life for clues. As early as 1859, Charles Darwin suggested that biological diversity (or biodiversity) is a clear sign of plant community health. Since then, evidence has shown that plant biodiversity does indeed help an ecosystem weather trauma and bounce back from natural disasters, such as fire or hurricane. If a forest's large trees are blown down in a hurricane, for instance, the understory plants—particularly those whose growth was held in check by the trees' presence—usually have a growth spurt and begin filling the open spaces. They provide wildlife with food and control erosion until seedlings become established and replace the trees that have fallen.

Only recently, a three-member team of scientists found in field experiments in Minnesota using native prairie plants that biological diversity helps plants make more efficient use of nutrients in the soil as well. That is, in test plots planted with many different kinds of prairie plants, the plants ate better, grew better, and covered the ground better than in less diverse test plots. The researchers also found that in the more diverse plots less nitrogen was lost from the soil through leaching. Nitrogen is one of the most important elements required for plant growth. The researchers concluded that greater nutrient use and less nitrogen loss help keep the soil fertile and allow the ecosystem to thrive. The experiments proved that, as Darwin predicted, biodiverse systems are healthier systems.

As Joni and Robin drafted a plan for the stretch of Natividad Creek that cuts through the park, they drew up long lists reflecting what historically had grown on its banks. They needed to encourage biological diversity to help return the wounded ecosystem to health, to draw birds and other wildlife back. The plants would be the beginning of Natividad Creek's recuperation.

It is only a few minutes before 9 a.m. Tricia and her volunteers have spent the last two hours unloading and placing plants beside the bamboo markers on the steep slope. Now she looks both pensive and tired as she assigns last-minute chores and coordinates the dozen or so volunteers. They include former teachers and current graduate students, plant aficionados and first-time planters. One young man named Sean, sporting a neatly trimmed dark beard and a Cleveland Indians cap, allows that he just happened to be visiting his sister and she dragged him along for the event.

Bruce Stewart troubleshoots glitches as they arise. In what

may be his most important task of the day, he borrows Ed's car phone and tracks down the whereabouts of a delivery of portable toilets, which, someone on the phone assures him, are on their way.

Tricia gathers the volunteers on a dirt-covered flat at the edge of the park's slope for final instructions. She points at the neatly arranged shovels, gloves, and empty white buckets to be distributed among the crews before they head down the slope. She explains the stakes and ribbons. A shrub for every stake, a stake for every shrub. She explains the planting sequence: "Trees first, grass second." Every group of children will have the chance to plant at least three bushes or a tree together. After that, the students can plant the grass plugs on their own. Trays of grasses in stubbies sit beside the supplies. The group of volunteers begins to break. Some stand around and wait; others organize their own pile of tools or collect stubbies. Tricia notices that one planting plot doesn't have a volunteer assigned to it. "Who wants to take this plot?" she calls out with a hint of urgency. "I need a volunteer for a plot."

"I will," a voice offers.

"What am I doing?" a volunteer asks.

"Saving the world," a wag responds. The quip is met by a burst of laughter from the group.

With the kind of rumble that school buses and cars without mufflers share, the first yellow chariot of children appears in the distance. Tricia realizes she needs to move her car, which is parked at the curb where the buses will unload. She passes her keys to a bystander. The Rabbit is packed with the daily accoutrements of student life: extra shoes, extra clothes, books, papers, reports.

"Look at the backseat of her car," jokes Ed Piper, pointing at Tricia's mobile closet. "That's all her possessions. She comes in one day and it's cold as heck out and she's got on socks and her sandals and Bruce Stewart says, 'Where are your shoes?' She says, 'Oh, they're in my car.' And I say, 'There's no need to say anything more, Trish.' " He pauses to watch the bus pull up to the curb.

He really enjoys the Return of the Natives crowd, he says. "They're all the type of people I relate to and I haven't found anybody [like that] for a long time." For instance, there's the volunteer who takes off a month at a time to backpack in the high Sierra. "Then she comes back and tells me about all these great experiences," Ed says, beaming. "One day I'll figure a way to get up there."

An outdoorsman, Ed has had to adapt his approach to nature to the crutches that help keep him mobile. When he was nineteen, during his second year of college, a car accident left him partially paralyzed. One of the first things he did when he was released from the hospital was to go duck hunting. His route took him through a swamp, and as he settled one crutch on the ground, it sank deep into the muck. It was no way to hunt, he decided. Since then, he has modified his outdoor activities, sticking to solid trails and using a four-wheel drive to take him into the back roads of California, Canada, and Colorado. "I've got a little Coleman tent trailer and a collapsible boat, all that stuff. My kids and I, we take off probably about five or six weeks a year camping." Today he will crisscross the park in his truck and watch from the driver's seat as it takes shape.

Another school bus and then another pulls up. Finally, when they are all parked, the doors open and children of all sizes stream out. Tiny first-graders follow fifth-graders, and the adult volunteers spring into action.

Cleveland Indians fan Sean collects a group of fourth- and fifth-graders from one bus and leads them to where the tools are. There are eleven boys and one girl in the group. "All right. I need two volunteers," Sean announces. Hands shoot up, and Sean selects two boys to carry a bucket filled with gloves and trowels and a flat of grasses. Then the crew wends its way down the slope to a midpoint where colored tape waves from sticks. The kids gather around Sean. He stands silent for a moment to capture their attention.

Sean holds up an acorn. "Does anybody know what grows from an acorn?"

Momentary silence and then a guess flies. "A tree."

"Okay," Sean agrees. "A tree does grow from an acorn. Anybody know what kind of trees?"

More guesses from the enthusiastic crew.

"Redwood."

"Pine."

"Acorn tree"—said with a giggle.

"Oak tree," a boy named David finally says with authority.

"An oak tree," Sean repeats, pleased. "David, all right."

"Daviiiiid," his pals offer in congratulations.

"Okay," Sean says to quiet the group. Today they will be planting trees on this slope, which is part of the new park. "It doesn't look too good now, does it?"

His followers offer their agreement. They seem prepared to chatter about the park-to-be's barren appearance, but Sean takes control again. "It looks bad right now because nobody cares about it and nobody's doing anything about it. What you guys are doing here today—you guys are going to be planting and taking care of the park. The plants that we're planting today are what are called native plants. What that means is that these are the plants that were here before people came and cut them down and poisoned them and built their houses all around here. So this whole area around here used to have all kinds of plants and trees, and all kinds of birds and animals used to live here. That's what we want: we want the birds to come back in. And the animals." He finishes by telling the crew that each time they come to the park in the future they will see the plants they planted and know they did something special. With that, he hands over stewardship of the park to these kids and their families.

Sean keeps the pace going, passing out tools and gloves. A boy named Roy, his thick jet-black hair suavely combed back, holds up hands already covered with black suede gloves. "I've come prepared," he says with cocky pride and a jaunty smile. "That's the kind of guy I am."

Three boys volunteer to take a bucket and fill it with mulch. The rest of Sean's group stays with him as he helps them plant three bushes that measure no higher than eight inches once they are tucked into the ground. All the students get a chance to do something. One digs, another loosens a plant from its pot, a third puts the plant in the ground and fills in the soil. Others make a basin, cover the soil with mulch, water. Then the group breaks into pairs. Kneeling in the soft, moist soil, the children chaotically pull weeds and then plug native grass tufts into the ground.

The pairs demonstrate varying degrees of care. One works with swift and delicate movements that make the process look more like surgery than like gardening. Another slaps the plug into the ground with unconcerned speed. Most of these children, though they live in a town surrounded by farmland, say they have not gardened or planted anything before. A few have helped their parents do yard work. All of them seem eager to contribute to this park's landscape.

After a hectic hour, the first shift of planters, muddier than when they arrived, marches up the slope and back into the buses. The Return of the Natives staff and volunteers seem relieved to have a few minutes to regroup before the next shift arrives. Sixty more students than originally scheduled came in the first shift, but the volunteers handled the extra arrivals without difficulty.

Joni drives up during the break, dressed in jeans and ready to work. She warmly greets Bruce and Tricia and the volunteers, most of them friends or acquaintances. Then she tours the slope alone, eager to get a close look at the planting before the next shift rolls in. She examines the arrangement of the stakes and the plants that are already in the ground. The massing doesn't look right to her. The larger shrubs look too scattered. The weeds, mostly various types of exotic grasses introduced over the decades for pasture and lawns, are higher than she realized. She worries that the young plants, especially the native grasses, won't be able to compete with the weeds. She had been to the park before, but not in the past week. "I think I should have been out here beforehand," she says as she surveys the slope. "I think I would have prescribed weed whipping."

A Return of the Natives volunteer calls to Joni from the top of the slope. Could she give an opinion on some holes he is trying to dig for trees on the park floor? She follows the volunteer, a burly man with a red beard who wears a floppy canvas hat to protect him from the overcast sun. He has been trying to use an auger, a tool that looks like a giant drill, to dig holes. But the park's floor has been so compacted by heavy equipment that the drill barely works in some spots. He has had to change some of the trees' positions by a couple of feet. Joni kicks her boot toe into the hard soil. It barely gives. She assures the volunteer he made the right move and that the new tree locations look fine.

Then she looks back up the slope twenty yards away and imagines what it will look like in a few years' time. She envisions a low-rise forest of grasses and shrubs, dense with leaves and color. She sees buckeyes blooming white in spring. She sees, eventually, an oak canopy shading portions of the slope. In her mind, she sees a beautiful landscape like that of the places she likes to hike on weekends.

Joni trudges up the slope just as another bus arrives. Tricia realizes she is short a volunteer and asks Joni to take on a group of children. Soon, the landscape architect is crouching on the slope, helping a dozen pint-size nouveau gardeners. This group is bilingual, and Spanish and English share air space. One shy boy who speaks little English concentrates on finding a suitable place for a single grass plug. He tugs on weeds until he decides the ground is clear enough, then digs a hole with a trowel, moving tablespoonfuls of dirt at a time. Holding a grass plug with delicate care, as though it were spun glass, he lowers it into the ground and tenderly pats soil into place. He plants two more plugs before he decides he has done enough. A few minutes later, the littlest gardener follows his classmates back on the bus and to school.

After the second round of children leave, Tricia, Bruce, Ed, and the Return of the Natives volunteers gather on the flat above the slope which has become their staging ground. They huddle over sack lunches of sandwiches, apples, and cookies and swap stories about the morning's events. Bruce asks Joni's assessment of the young planters' work. She pauses for a moment before answering. She doesn't want to discourage the group, but she knows the planting arrangement is not perfect. In a more typical situation, a landscape contractor with a crew of experienced adult workers would be responsible for putting in the plants. Every hole would be dug to the right depth, every root covered with the right amount of soil. If anything didn't meet a standard, the landscape architect would point out flaws and expect improvement. Joni understands, though, that this project has other strengths.

The volunteers may need to go over the area later to make sure all the plants have the right amount of soil cover, she says. She noticed some grass plugs that still had roots exposed. They may also need to add more mulch to some plants. But, she quickly adds, the children's work is really exciting and a good thing.

This is just the first planting day, and by its end, 474 children will have contributed their labor to the park. There will be another planting tomorrow, and then several more over the coming year. On some days, adults and whole families will join the schoolchildren. Eventually, oaks and coffeeberry, buckeyes and monkey flowers will cover the slope and the bank of the ditch-like span of creek below. Sedges and rushes and wildflowers will fill the barren spots at the wild end of the creek. It will be greener and more alive than it has been in years. It will be the children's handmade paradise.

Over the years, people have given Joni sets of Guatemalan worry dolls. Tradition says the tiny woven figures, so small a dozen fit into a hand-size basket, will carry away any worries they are assigned. Lately, Joni feels that she could do a lot of assigning.

Within a few days' time, she has to present the first fully thought out Hewlett-Packard landscape design to what the company is calling the landscape's "customers." The customers, in this case, are representatives of various company divisions whose members will look out on and walk through the new landscape each workday. Over the last few weeks, at smaller meetings, the committee overseeing the project has requested additions to her firm's original design. Could she add a water element? Could she extend the plan to include another courtyard?

Incorporating these requests into the design has been no problem. But she knows they will add to the project's overall cost. And she worries that cost estimates will come in far over what HP has budgeted. She has tried cutting some expenses by stretching the savanna to cover more parking area and pulling in the woodlands. But she doesn't think those savings will compensate for the additions.

Meanwhile, she has prepared her cost estimates for the Sands' landscape. As they requested, she has broken the plan into phases. The hardscape skeleton and boundaries make up the first phase. She recommends first laying the driveway, the main stone walk to the front door, and the four porches, one for each side of the house. She also recommends building the front gate and wall in the first phase to increase the family's privacy immediately.

Softscape dominates the second phase. This calls for putting in most of the plants and irrigation. In the third phase, she suggests finishing the remaining hardscaping, including some patios and walkways, putting in a garden shed, and creating the secret niche, a small hideaway with a pottery fountain. In the fourth and final phase, she includes the pool, spa, pool house, pergola, arbor, and play court.

To do a first round of estimates on a project, a landscape architect works from the paper plan, measuring each area and converting the square inches to square feet. Then, using a combination of experience, price lists, and standard schedules that show typical construction costs, the architect figures the cost per square foot of materials (e.g., paving stones, cement) and their installation. Joni assigned Michael the task of collecting numbers for the Sands project.

When she first eyeballed the Sands' homestead, Joni figured it would cost more than $250,000 to landscape it. Michael's more detailed estimates came in at about $370,000. The final phase, with the pool and pool house, was the most expensive, nearly $150,000. The first phase, the one the

Sands would have to think about doing sooner rather than later, would cost about $82,000. Joni built in a ten-percent contingency to cover unknown or unexpected costs. Depending on what materials the Sands choose for the hardscape, the project could cost more or less.

Dennis and Abbe are anxious to get the front wall and gate done. Already, they have had a call from a real estate agent who read their lack of landscaping as a sign that the couple had come upon hard times and would be willing to sell their dream house for a song. "I expressed my annoyance that she called," Dennis says with understated calm a few weeks later. All the other houses on the block have shrubs or fences blocking an easy view into the yard. "Now we know why," Dennis observes.

One late Thursday afternoon, Joni hurries to the post office to mail the Sands the completed phasing plan. When she returns to her office, there is a message from Abbe on the answering machine. The Sands have decided to postpone all landscape work. It seems more urgent now to install a French drain system around the house to help direct rainwater away from the newly repaired foundation.

The news disappoints Joni. Designing a landscape without seeing it completed is doing only half a job. Each delay makes her worry that she won't get to see the finished work.

The Sands haven't abandoned the landscaping, though. They figure they will start working on it in the summer, half a year away. "We've taken the approach with this whole thing that we're not pushing it. We're not trying to rush through anything. We're not in any hurry," Dennis says. "We've found, for us, what has always worked the best, particularly for things that we know little about, like landscaping, is to take as much time as we can to think it over and ultimately do the right thing. It's very easy to make very expensive mistakes, things that you just regret. We've never regretted being patient."

IX

TOM COURTRIGHT'S NURSERY IS A VISUAL CARnival. Stylish garden furniture decorates outdoor "rooms" that line the front of the long, single-story main building. There are sturdy wrought-iron chairs and teak tables pretty enough to grace a dining room.

Inside, garden-theme decorations share shelf space with fancy pruners and specialty fertilizers packed in bags, boxes, and bottles. Metal frogs and fish burble water in a working fountain display. Handsome pottery is spread like interior-design accents throughout the store. Floral wreaths hang on walls. Everything is tasteful and pretty. Even the neatly kept shelves that hold insecticides look colorful, inviting. There is no stench of manure here, no eau de pesticide.

Out the back door that opens onto an expanded patio, plants provide sweet fragrance and splashes of color under the summer sun. Hundreds of potted plants surround a fountain, creating an elegant giant centerpiece. In the background is the sound of moving water. Perennials are here, annuals are there, arranged in sections according to type, in a space about the size of half a city block.

It is 8 a.m. and a customer is cruising down the long sloping driveway that leads from a busy suburban street into the garden center's parking lot. She passes a well-ordered forest of potted trees and a two-story Spanish-style home that now serves as a gift shop. She parks close to Orchard Nursery & Florist's main building and hurries through its unlocked doors, heading directly for the checkout counter. No one is there, but the woman is not discouraged. Dressed in pressed white slacks and blue-striped knit shell, she passes time by wandering down an aisle, examining garden trinkets. Courtright, a big man with sharp blue eyes and cropped wavy brown hair, appears from a hallway behind the counter. He seems surprised to see her, but she has been lying in wait and rattles off her requirements. She needs to pick up a wreath she put on hold yesterday. And, oh, yes, she wants four bags of medium-size bark.

"We're not open until 9 a.m., ma'am. Nobody's here to load," Courtright says, firmly dismissing the request for bark. He is mildly annoyed. He has been on the phone for much of the last half hour, trying to straighten out logistical details for a busload of French nursery owners and managers touring California garden centers. They will be here in two hours. He feels harried but remains calm and tracks down the woman's wreath. He rings it up with a few metal plant hangers the customer found while she waited. Total sale: $73.84. And the store hasn't opened yet.

Orchard Nursery abuts a freeway just outside the center of Lafayette, a hilly, well-to-do suburb about fifteen minutes' drive east of Oakland. Two nurserymen opened it in 1946 and by the late 1960s the business was among the most upscale nurseries in the San Francisco Bay Area. In the late 1960s and early 1970s, Courtright would occasionally drive out from Berkeley, where he grew up working in his father's nursery. "I was always impressed by the cars that were in the parking lot, even in those days. Coming from Berkeley, where we had to deal with all the hippies and free spirits in the world, to come out and see Mercedes and Porsches and things like that, that was a pretty nice change."

Armed with a horticulture degree, Courtright bought Orchard on Independence Day in 1972. He has built it into what nursery industry insiders cite as a fine example of a full-service, independent garden center—the trade's name for a retail nursery—that uses up-to-date retailing techniques. Department-store-style merchandising meets plant selling at Orchard Nursery, and customers keep flowing in and buying. They complete about a hundred thousand transactions a year that amount to more than $4.5 million.

Even the most reluctant gardener relies at some point on a retail nursery to help dress a landscape. Garden centers like Courtright's have a huge influence on what goes into the everyday landscape, the landscape that people plant themselves in their own yards. Landscape architects like Joni Janecki, who attempt to introduce clients to native plants and concepts such as plant communities, often find themselves struggling against the power and influence of garden centers.

Garden centers can shape what we see in our neighborhoods just by what they choose to sell in their shops. What they choose to sell in their shops reflects a complex combination of factors. Employees' personal tastes, the customers' wants, gardening trends that originate from various sources, nursery industry traditions, and, increasingly, the power of savvy advertising, all have an influence. So, too, does the simple desire to survive as a viable business.

Courtright enjoys plants, but he enjoys retail even more. He loves selling.

"The real challenge is getting people to visit the garden centers. We're always looking for stuff—different things people can add to their yards," he explains as he leads a visitor through his business's plant collection. "I hate to use the word circus, but we're setting a stage. We're continually setting the stage and the whole idea is to get the customer to come back more often. That's the real challenge as far as retailing goes."

Courtright pauses to call out a request to an employee who is straightening up a plant display. "Hey, Karen, the pot by your left foot has a price on the side." Karen directs her attention to a dark green leafy plant in a black plastic one-gallon pot, then turns the pot slightly to hide its price from immediate view.

Price is a difficult issue for independent garden centers like Courtright's. Where once only independent nurseries existed to sell plants to homeowners, now just about every kind of store sells plants. Customers can buy plants at the grocery store and the drugstore. The mass merchandisers like Wal-Mart and Home Depot include sizable garden centers within their superstores. When it comes to price, independents like Courtright's Orchard clearly can't go head-to-head with the big national chains. A store like Courtright's sells plants at about two and a half times the wholesale price. In contrast, a giant merchandiser sells plants at just twice the wholesale price, and sometimes much less. Moreover, the big merchandisers buy in such volume that they usually pay a lower wholesale price per plant.

In the nursery industry, labor costs typically average 16 to 18 percent of total costs. A large chain's labor costs can account for just 6 percent of the total cost of doing business. Courtright has forty full-time employees and a dozen part-timers in his shop, and with health benefits and profit-sharing, he pays a higher wage than normal in this generally low-paying industry. His labor costs account for nearly 28 percent of his total costs. All this means he can't sell his plants for the same bargain prices the big chains can.

Nevertheless, independent nurseries continue to draw customers and make money. Some, like Homestead Gardens in Maryland and Bachman's in Minneapolis, have become almost legendary for their ability to keep customers coming through their doors. Many weekends they are packed with people, almost year-round despite shorter growing seasons in the Northern climates. Measured by sales, the mass merchandisers like Home Depot, Kmart, and Wal-Mart dominate a list of the top hundred nursery retailers. Each of these department stores sells hundreds of times more than the typical independent. Yet three-fourths of the top hundred are independent garden centers, and some thirty operate with just one or two stores. Add to this the thousands of much smaller nurseries scattered around the country that never make it even close to the top-hundred list but still manage to keep afloat.

How do these independents do it? They figure if they can't compete head-to-head with the big merchandisers on price, they must distinguish themselves in other ways. One way is by staying ahead of trends in nonliving garden items. That's one of the reasons Courtright's dry-goods department carries high-priced water garden equipment, fancy hose hangers, garden-theme gifts and clothes. "It used to be you were selling 90 percent plants and 10 percent other," Courtright explains. Now he estimates that half the money his store collects in sales comes from garden furniture.

Despite this, Courtright insists that plants remain the priority at his nursery. Knowing and keeping up with plant trends is essential to attracting customers who will spend money on plants and garden equipment. "Quality and selection are the key," says Peter Tourtellotte, Orchard's plant buyer. Where the big chain might offer a single yellow variety of yarrow, for instance, Orchard sells six different varieties representing a rainbow of colors. It strives to be a place where shoppers can find new ideas, new information, new products, and new varieties of plants. It tries to cultivate and feed gardening consumers' drive to want more. "We're getting people in here and we're telling them what they want for the most part," Tourtellotte says. "We're inspiring them to want something with the displays and the quality."

More than just about anyone else at the nursery, Tourtellotte directly influences what plants will be available to the store's customers and what will show up in the everyday landscape in the fifteen-mile radius the nursery serves. A slender thirty-something man, Tourtellotte looks scholarly in wire-rimmed spectacles and neatly trimmed light brown beard. A plant lover since his teens, he earned a degree in horticulture, expecting to work with plants as interior-design elements. But after college he worked in a nursery and found that he liked the business. Now, at Orchard, his job means keeping on top of what's new in gardening and trying to stock the nursery with plants his customers want, even if they don't realize they want them until they step through Orchard's doors.

From Sunday through Tuesday, Tourtellotte spends most of his workday at his desk in the functional office he shares with two others in a boxy building behind the main shop. During that three-day period, as many as fifty sales representatives from wholesale growers visit Tourtellotte, bringing with them long lists of products. The large national wholesalers come in on Sunday. The smaller local and regional growers' representatives, including a couple of native-plant growers, come in the following two days. Tuesday is dominated by wholesalers who specialize in perennials, including some back-yard growers from Lafayette. Later in the week, trucks roll up to deliver the plants and Tourtellotte makes sure someone inspects the delivery and confirms that plants are healthy, looking their best. "We return a lot of material if it isn't up to snuff," he says.

On one Tuesday morning, Tourtellotte holds up an inch-thick sheaf of papers, all printed in single-spaced type. These are just two days' worth of plant availability lists he has collected from sales reps. He usually reads a rep's list during his visit and knows immediately what he wants. "You get very quick about reading availabilities," he says.

Tourtellotte pulls the list from Hines Nurseries from the pile to demonstrate. It is about fifteen pages long. "When I get to junipers, I can go right past them," he says with amusement as he flips past three pages, each line representing a different variety of the common evergreen. "We have the fortunate situation of not really having to sell junipers."

A popular regional garden book describes junipers as "the most widely used woody plants" in the Western United States. They are often planted in solid masses to fill corners of yards, cover parkway strips, hide house foundations, and once they gain age and size, they hide whole houses. Among many landscape architects, designers, and gardening sophisticates, junipers have become objects of derision. "They got overdone," Tourtellotte explains.

Junipers are hardy plants that come in tree, shrub, or groundcover forms and don't require a green thumb. They are usually a solid shade of green, but some varieties have butter-yellow highlights on branch tips. The plants remain standard stock in a lot of mainstream nurseries and are especially valued by gardeners in snowy climates who want to introduce color into winter landscapes. At Orchard Nursery, customers don't have to worry about snow and are hardly limited by climate. Tourtellotte and his colleagues have tried subtly to change the way their customers think about junipers by showing them planted singly with other plants in displays. "They really can be nice songs when they're not planted in huge masses," Tourtellotte says.

The plant availability lists that get the most attention from

Tourtellotte are those for perennials, particularly flowering perennials. Perennials are plants that live for more than two years, usually have nonwoody stems, and have flowers. In contrast, shrubs have woody stems and last for many years, and annuals last just one season. Sometimes the aboveground part of a perennial plant dies back during the winter, but its roots remain alive and the plant reappears in the spring. Sedum, hostas, and daylilies are perennials. Junipers and pittosporum, pansies and petunias are not.

Several factors have contributed to the popularity of perennials since the mid-1980s. Fewer people move into new, unlandscaped homes now, and those who do have smaller yards than home buyers did decades ago. The result: consumers buy fewer big trees and large woody shrubs to fill expansive yards. They want compact plants to fit smaller spaces.

Also, more people live in homes that have already been landscaped. "Ten years ago, these were all container shrubs," Courtright says as he sweeps his arms across rows and columns of perennials in his nursery. "But the shrubbery isn't selling for us. We don't have a lot of new homes in this area. People are just redoing their yards, adding this and adding that." The this and that they turn to more and more are flowering perennials.

Finally, even though surveys show that gardening is currently one of America's favorite outdoor leisure activities, retailers like Courtright and Tourtellotte know most of their customers have dozens of distractions vying for their free time. Spending weekends doing tedious yard maintenance has less appeal when there are children to entertain, mountains to bike, waters to paddle, movies to see, and computers to tame. Homeowners want instant gardens. Annuals like pansies and impatiens still provide a lot of the immediate color, but perennials have gained as consumers decide they want the flowers without having to replant every season.

Home and life-style changes haven't been the only boon to perennials. High-profile use by high-profile landscape designers has helped promote them, too. Landscape architects James Van Sweden and Wolfgang Oehme, a prominent Washington, D.C., team, helped heighten the status of perennials in the late 1970s and early 1980s when they used them in richly colored and varied landscape designs. They included unusual ornamental grasses that were largely unknown in contemporary American gardens.

Also, perennial plant growers themselves have actively promoted interest in their product. In the mid-1980s, they organized a trade group to help keep perennials in the garden news. Now the organization publishes a quarterly journal and annually conducts surveys about which perennials sell the best. Among the most popular and consistent sellers are the big-leafed shade-loving hostas, daylilies of various sorts, chrysanthemums, sedum, ornamental grasses, coreopsis, phlox, various coneflowers, and astilbe, sometimes called meadowsweet.

The perennial-growers group also selects one perennial each year to promote to garden writers and nurseries around the country. The plant has to have good color and good form and be fairly easy to grow to win the designation. Nursery buyers like Tourtellotte report that customers snap up an all-but-ignored perennial variety after it has won a perennial-of-the-year designation. In 1995 it was blue-flowered Russian sage. In 1996 it was a red-flowered penstemon variety developed at the University of Nebraska, where it was dubbed Husker Red.

Utimately, the thing that draws customers to a plant, whether it be a perennial or a shrub, is its flowers. Tourtellotte has found that when the plants in the nursery's own permanent landscape come into bloom, requests for them soar. Each week, when he orders plants, he focuses on the ones that are flowering or are in bud.

Leaning back in his desk chair, Tourtellotte holds up another thick stack of paper. Each page bears special orders from customers. The nursery gets up to eighty such requests a week. Tourtellotte can almost track what plants are in bloom in public landscapes based on the requests. "Jacarandas are happening right now because down on the corridor to San Jose they're in full bloom and everybody wants them," he says. In the next town over, a landscape architect has included bush anemone, a California native, in a museum's landscape. When its cloud-white blossoms unfold, nursery customers begin asking for it. Public landscapes influence what people buy, but with a laugh and a shrug, Tourtellotte concludes, "Color is what drives this business, that's all there is to it."

Some horticulturists and landscape architects groan about the flower passion. They complain that customers and clients are too often disappointed in any plant that doesn't flower with almost garish intensity or unnatural abundance. The subtler plants, including many native plants, get left behind in favor of the nursery world's version of polyester plaid.

Plant selection and breeding programs have become more sophisticated as the nursery industry has grown. Flowering plants have become more available. Whether this availability has followed or led the flower passion is hard to know. Whatever the case, the typical flowers found in landscapes have gotten bigger, brighter, and more profuse. And if, as some garden writers contend, white flowers are highest in gardening's color hierarchy, then plebeian tastes have taken over. Just about anything other than white, from reds to purples to yellows to pinks, sells better.

One queen of the flowering plants in the nursery industry is neither a perennial nor an annual, but a shrub. It is the rose.

Orchard Nursery's rose-selling season is relatively short, focused mostly on spring before the summer temperatures soar to the 100-degree range. Hot weather plays havoc with roses and makes it hard to keep this garden center's potted plants looking nice. By mid-June, the rose inventory is down to a few dozen. But even with the short season, Courtright and his faithful crew will sell about six thousand rosebushes.

Traditionally, the biggest-selling roses in this country have been the shrub roses, specimen plants that stand like floral sentries, stiff and separate from others in the garden. In the 1980s, some rose companies started promoting landscape roses. These are social roses, growing together in flowing masses as thick hedges or groundcover. While rose-savvy gardeners were aware of landscape roses, the average gardener—and especially the reluctant gardener whose trips to nurseries are usually brief and painfully awkward—was mostly oblivious.

Then came the Ground Cover Rose Flower Carpet Pink, Var. Noatraum. Note the capital letters: this rose's name is a trademark. Not just any pink rose, according to its promoters, it is disease- and mildew-resistant, so it doesn't require lots of pesticides. It doesn't need fancy pruning, flowers ten months of the year, and is flexible enough to be used as a lawn substitute or a potted plant. Its proud purveyors call it the "environmental rose" and a "new-generation, easy-care, eco-rose." It is, if you trust the labeling's claims, one rosa perfecta.

The patented rose went on sale in the United States for the first time in 1995. Within a month, retail nurseries ordered more than a million and sold them faster than they could keep them in stock. The rose's promoters expected to sell more than two million within the first eighteen months. In fact, within the first nine months, customers snapped up more than 2.2 million. To put this in perspective, consider that a typical new rose from one of the large rose companies might sell a tenth as many in the first year.

Flower Carpet must be an amazing plant, more wonderful than any other plant available, right? Well, it does come with an amazing advertising campaign that has caught the attention of just about any alert person in the nursery industry. This campaign may be an anomaly or it may be a sign of what's to come as modern marketing takes hold of the historically marketing-passive nursery industry. It plays to people's desire to have pretty flowers without spending a lot of time in the garden. It also plays to a decreasing interest in pesticides, something nurserymen like Courtright have witnessed as pesticide sales have spiraled down in garden centers. Finally, the Flower Carpet and its advertising campaign benefit from consumers' interest in planting in their garden whatever is new and unusual. It is a good example of how to sell a single plant nationwide almost overnight.

In a photograph in Flower Carpet literature, Werner Noack, a grandfatherly-looking rose breeder dressed in suspenders and a wide-brimmed hat, kneels, tenderly displaying one of the prize roses. Noack spent twenty-five years at his growing grounds in Germany, trying to produce a rose plant that would be virtually care-free, low-growing, and full of flowers, according to its promoters. The work paid off with the Flower Carpet.

In 1989, after patenting the plant in Europe, obtaining complete control over who could propagate and sell it there, Noack entered the rose in top European rose competitions, where it received awards and good reviews. He also started offering the plant on a modest scale in Germany and Holland. Then he sent it to a large distributor in Canada on a trial basis to see how well it would sell there. Enter Anthony Tesslar, an Australian bulb grower with a knack for marketing, who learned about the rose from the Canadian distributor. Tesslar saw a potential Australian hit. He obtained distribution rights from Noack, created a marketing plan for Australia and New Zealand, and signed on Australian growers to produce the plant. Just as he hoped, the Flower Carpet rose sold big, and he moved the campaign to Europe, South Africa, and England. Finally, it came to the United States.

Traditionally, in the nursery industry, wholesale growers have marketed to retailers and then left it up to retailers to do what needs to be done to sell plants to consumers. The Flower Carpet campaign deviates from that system with a marketing strategy that goes directly from the producer to the consumer and doesn't rely on retailers to come up with ways to sell the plant.

In the United States, Tesslar hired Dan Davids, a California bulb wholesaler, to run the marketing program under the Flower Carpet USA banner. Davids lined up eight wholesalers to grow the plant according to set guidelines and then distribute it across the country. In exchange for a royalty of $2 per plant, the wholesalers obtained the right to grow and sell the rose. They also enjoyed the benefit of a national advertising campaign that picks up each spring.

In its first year, Flower Carpet promoters in the United States spent $2 million on marketing. That included full-page ads in nursery trade magazines to tout the rose, followed by a public-relations campaign directed at garden writers around the country. The Flower Carpet company gave some of the most influential journalists and garden magazines sample plants to test in their gardens months before the shipping date of the first plants. "We believe the editorial is far more important than the paid advertising," Davids says. The strategy paid off immediately. Garden writers around the country produced favorable columns and radio and television broadcasts about the rose. But the Flower Carpet organization didn't ignore paid consumer advertising. To the contrary, when the plant actually went on sale in garden centers, the company bought full-page ads in the most widely read home and garden magazines, including *Sunset* in the West and *Southern Living* in the Southeast.

The marketing plan didn't stop there. It also covered the

rose's packaging and method of release. There are several Flower Carpet rose colors, but to enhance the plant's cachet and keep interest and sales up, the Flower Carpet companies release only one color a year in their respective countries. Pink was released first, followed by white, and, later, red. In the first release, each pink Flower Carpet rose plant came packed in a pink plastic pot that would coordinate with, say, a pink plastic-flamingo garden ornament. Each pot bore the Flower Carpet emblem and each plant carried a label with planting instructions, and a small packet of rose food.

"It's part of taking what I would consider brand-marketing techniques à la Coca Cola or Campbell Soup and applying them to a plant—which has never been done before—and taking it to the market," explains Davids. "That does a number of things. It helps keep your product proprietary and it makes it very easily recognizable for the consumer out in the marketplace."

Just two months after the first Flower Carpet release in the United States, a man and a woman approaching retirement age were strolling amid a huge crowd at the Los Angeles Garden Show, a five-day feast of gardening lectures, sometimes garish table-setting displays, and elaborate designed landscapes. The annual show resembles dozens held around the country to promote fine taste—and big spending—in the garden, while raising money for some good cause. As the couple examined a children's garden of coneflowers and daisies, the man turned to his companion and asked, "That rose they're advertising everywhere, have you tried that?"

She shook her head, exclaiming, "I looked at it, but it costs $15!"

Only minutes later, four well-dressed elderly women stood at another landscape display a few feet away and approvingly considered dozens of colorful perennials, towering red cannas, and a banana tree. One noticed low-growing pink rose plants at the display's edge. "Isn't that that new Carpet rose?" she asked the most horticulturally knowledgeable member of the group. "Yes, it's a new plant. It's very popular in Europe," the expert replied, then added proudly, "I've got three of them. I've got them in pots."

The rose was the buzz.

When it comes to Flower Carpet, Davids doesn't want to stop at the back-yard gardener. He has started placing ads in magazines targeted at landscape architects and the public-agency employees who make public-landscape decisions. His aim is to get Flower Carpet roses into public landscapes across the country, from highway medians to county parks. Imagine that: one big country, wall-to-wall in Flower Carpet.

X

IN CONTEMPORARY AMERICAN CULTURE, PLANTS share a position similar to most foods. We know where to buy them, but we rarely know much about how they got there. Yet the getting there has a profound impact on what is available to buy, what is available to plant in our landscapes. Until now, most plants have had a much slower introduction into the Western world's landscape than has the Flower Carpet rose. Most have followed a quieter, although no less complicated, route to the store shelf.

The traditional route a plant takes from its natural habitat to the nursery shelf begins with explorers, botanists, plant researchers, breeders, and propagators. It moves to growers and wholesale nursery owners who decide what would be fun and profitable to grow. It ends with the buyers, such as Orchard Nursery's Peter Tourtellotte, who select what plants to sell in the retail nurseries and home-improvement stores, all the while hoping they have accurately judged their customers' tastes and buying habits.

The route is like a chain of increasingly narrow funnels stacked one atop another. It is the widest at the top, where the explorers, researchers, and breeders stand, and the narrowest at the bottom, where the retail buyers and their customers wait. Only a fraction of the plants started on the route actually get past all the funnels and into the created landscape. Of those, an even smaller fraction are plants native to the typical retail nursery's region. From early in Western gardening history, the funnels have favored exotics.

For ornamental plants, that history began in the early seventeenth century, when what one plant historian describes as a minor revolution hit England and Europe. Until then, Europeans and the colonists in North America gardened exclusively for food and for medicinal purposes. They grew apples to eat, herbs to cure disease. But, by the early 1600s, European commerce was booming. One result was increasing wealth among merchants and landlords, and some of that wealth went into gardening for pleasure. The profession of gardener was born and wealthy patrons commissioned the new professionals to design and plant their estates.

Among the first and most famous of these early professional ornamental gardeners was an English father-and-son team both of whom were named John Tradescant. The Tradescants and their clients tired quickly of the plants available locally and wanted to decorate their gardens with unusual plants from other parts of the world. Europeans, particularly the English, had heard reports about wonderful plants that grew in the new colonies across the Atlantic. So the Tradescants' clients sent the gardeners to North America to collect seeds and cuttings to bring back and grow into their nursery stock in England. In their own London garden, the Tradescants "eagerly brought together a unique living collection of exotic plants, tapping every possible source and using all the connections available to them to acquire and continuously augment it," noted Stephen Spongberg in *A Reunion of Trees*, his history of the introduction of exotic plants.

By the mid-1600s, enthusiasm for exotic plants had spread across Europe faster than a bad case of leaf rust. Gardeners, botanists, and adventure junkies traveled and traded and hunted for new plants from Asia and North America. Meanwhile, in North America's new colonies, gardeners imported familiar European plants as they simultaneously explored the new continent's plant bounty.

In the eighteenth and nineteenth centuries especially, plant enthusiasts in the settled Eastern United States wanted to know what was growing in the wilder Midwest and the newly opened West. Government teams sent to explore the new territories usually included somebody to collect plants and seeds and carry or send them home. Thomas Jefferson saw to it that Meriwether Lewis had special instructions in botany before Lewis and William Clark set out on their famous expedition through the Northwest.

Meanwhile, European explorers continued to cover the globe, including the United States, to find plants that would do well at home. These trips were not without danger. The explorers—typically, sponsored by government agencies, universities, botanic gardens, and occasionally nurseries—faced harsh climates, difficult terrain, unbroken trails, and, sometimes, hostile inhabitants.

One Scottish plant explorer, David Douglas, made three

long trips for the Horticultural Society of London in the 1820s and 1830s. The trips took him to Washington, Oregon, and California, where he discovered, among other plants, the Douglas fir and the Douglas iris. He spent long days in rugged country. "At the end of a day of collecting, it was not unusual for Douglas to find himself wet to the skin, suffering from an infected knee, and worrying about his deteriorating eyesight," notes Karen Nilsson in *A Wild Flower by Any Other Name*. Douglas's collecting came to a tragic end when he fell into an open pit in Hawaii where a wild bull was trapped. The bull gored to death the thirty-five-year-old explorer.

Today, botanic gardens, government agencies, universities, and nurseries continue to sponsor collecting trips to other regions and other countries. To varying degrees, each of these types of institutions is also involved in trying to get new plants into the general nursery market.

Sometimes, getting a new plant into the landscape amounts to little more than simply exposing growers and retailers to plants they have not previously considered growing and selling. At the North Carolina State University Arboretum, founder J. C. Raulston ran one of the most active programs of introduction through exposure. On a relatively modest budget, Raulston, a devotee of plant diversity in the landscape, spent almost every weekend and occasionally longer periods traveling in the United States and abroad, collecting plant seeds and cuttings from just about every source imaginable, including private gardens and small, out-of-the-way nurseries. He tried to grow much of what he collected, and what grew successfully ended up in the arboretum. Then he encouraged nursery owners and growers to visit with clipppers and coolers to take cuttings from the mature plants to build their own nursery stock. Raulston was credited with introducing literally thousands of plants to North Carolina's nursery industry, including native plants that hadn't previously been widely used in created landscapes.

Sometimes a plant is introduced into the nursery market deliberately in the hope of new profits. This is where wholesale plant growers come in.

On the edge of a sprawling Southern California suburb, five hundred acres of farmland sit snug against tracts of beige stucco homes. Rows and columns of black plastic pots, each one bearing a young plant, cover the farmland. These grounds are part of Hines Nurseries and the plants here represent just a fraction of the 1,500 different kinds that the company grows on four growing grounds totalling more than 1,400 acres, located in three states. One nursery trade magazine that tracks revenues in an industry whose main players are still largely privately owned estimates that Hines is the largest wholesale grower in the country. The company ships its plants all over the United States, supplying retail nurseries of just about every size and shape. Hines is to the nursery industry what IBM is to the computer industry, or Mattel is to the toy industry.

Thousands of other smaller wholesale nurseries grow and sell plants, but only a few do it on Hines's scale. Just like IBM, Hines continues to produce certain basic plants that are always in demand, the trees and shrubs that never seem to go out of style. But to stay competitive, to keep retail nursery buyers interested in ordering from its catalogue, Hines also has to continue developing and adding new plants and improving the old ones. "Our customers like new things," explains the company's new products coordinator, John Burke. "They like that change, the excitement of it."

Burke, soft-spoken, well-mannered, and trained in horticulture, is charged with making sure that new plants come into Hines. When the work goes well, the plants Burke squires into the company ultimately end up on store shelves and in landscapes all over. Burke's biggest challenge is finding those new plants.

Wholesale nurseries rely on a network of relationships to help find good plants. Burke, for instance, keeps in touch with a loose group of gardeners, independent horticulturists, industry consultants, and others scattered around the globe. When one of these freelancers comes upon an eye-catching plant that seems out of the ordinary, the finder alerts Burke. A new plant can be something as simple as a shrub in a corner of a botanical garden that had previously gone unnoticed by the nursery industry. Or it might be a peculiar variety that a garden hobbyist or plant professional has worked years to perfect through selection and breeding.

Hines employees also occasionally develop new varieties in the company's own fields. The company introduced new varieties of nandina, a bush with a bamboo-like appearance, after employees found interesting individuals in its fields of seed-grown plants. One benefit of planting a field of plants from seed is that almost all of them will be essentially identical, but slight genetic mutations will throw into the mix a few plants with different characteristics—an individual might, say, have a brighter flower color or a smaller leaf. When the mutations are attractive, growers can get to work propagating more of the unusual plant, typically by growing from cuttings, which become identical versions of the unusual plant.

Once a new plant turns up, Burke decides whether it has the charisma and timing of a good seller. That decision takes into account trends in landscaping and consumer buying. For instance, if retail nurseries have had lots of requests for plants with big leaves, astute wholesale growers stay alert for plants with big leaves. If Burke decides a new plant might sell, he and his staff try to learn as much about it as possible. They test how well it grows in various conditions, what kind of soil, climate, and watering regimen it needs, and how best to reproduce it.

Plants that are fast and easy to propagate—that is, plants that a grower can easily reproduce in quantity—have a better chance of making it to market. It can take a grower anywhere from several months to five years, sometimes longer, to test a plant fully. Growers usually feel more comfortable gambling on one that is easily propagated.

Most of the big wholesale growers consider several hundred plants each year. "What passes through our nursery can be an astounding number, but what's accepted is something else," says Burke. "We figure if we get one out of ten plants that is a keeper, a plant we want to grow, we're doing pretty well."

Tens of thousands of different species and varieties of plants are sold in this country. The average retail nursery can carry only several hundred at any one time. The nursery trade has to make room for new plants that will keep gardening interest up. A plant that growers or retailers do not believe will sell doesn't get into stores. If a plant gets into stores and then fails to sell well, it eventually disappears from the trade.

For the most part, the nursery industry, whose history and culture favor whatever is new and exotic, has not embraced native plants or their fans. Large mainstream growers carry few, if any, clearly identified native plants. At most mainstream retailers like Orchard, special native-plant sections are either rare or small, although buyers like Tourtellotte keep some common natives on hand and special-order others for customers.

The nursery industry has put comparatively little effort into identifying and propagating native varieties that meet a wide range of landscape requirements, with some notable exceptions. The Southern magnolia tree, for instance, has been heavily selected and bred to adapt to a plethora of growing conditions. Generally, though, it is up to local, specialized wholesale nurseries and specialized botanic gardens to find and cultivate garden-friendly natives.

Affection for native plants has waxed and waned in America's garden history. Their popularity and the advocacy of their use seem to cycle every other generation or so. In recent years, interest is on the rise, in conjunction with a rising interest in environmental protection and wildlands conservation. New native-plant wholsale nurseries have started up and succeeded. A handful of annual conferences in the East and Southeast that celebrate native plants sell out. The number of gardening how-to books that focus on using natives has grown. Garden magazines that once ignored natives entirely now include them, at least occasionally. In recent years, nursery trade magazines include more information about how to incorporate natives into the created landscape. Even trend-setting tastemaker Martha Stewart includes native plants in her repertoire.

One prominent landscape architect who uses native plants recalls that when her firm first started in 1975 she and her partners avoided mentioning native plants to clients. "The clients would say, 'We want rare and unusual plants,' and we said, 'The plants we're going to give you are so rare and unusual they're going to knock your socks off,' " recounts Carol Franklin of Andropogon Associates in Philadelphia. Then the firm would design a landscape of plants native to the local watershed. "They'd never seen them before, and they loved them. Because if you look at a sassafras or a marshmallow, these are knock-your-socks-off plants. But the horticultural trade had never focused on them. They were still into breeding a black rose, or the four-thousandth orchid or azalea or some flower as big as grapefruit. No one had bothered to see how beautiful much of what we have out there is."

These days Franklin barely has to sell the native-plant idea to clients. They come to her specifically asking for native plants and natural-looking landscapes. Finding local natives in nurseries has become easier, too. "When we started, it wasn't possible. There was a list of ten plants, and that's what the nurseries grew. It was like going to the supermarket and finding ten things on the shelf and they were all cans of tuna fish," Franklin says. "Nowadays, it's just completely different. And I think you have to have lived in those days to appreciate it."

Yet the recent increase in native-plant growers and aficionados hasn't meant a superabundance of native plants on the market. There are about 15,000 species of plants native to North America, excluding Mexico. This number doesn't include plants of a single species that have unusual characteristics which might qualify them in the nursery world for selection as a cultivated variety. Yet one would be hard-pressed to find more than a few hundred regional natives in even specialty native-plant nurseries. The time, effort, and money that the American nursery industry and garden-related organizations have poured into developing garden-worthy exotics has not been matched for native plants.

Ironically, it is easier to find many North American natives in European gardens than it is to find them here. Dick Lighty, director of the Mt. Cuba Center for the Study of Piedmont Flora, a private garden in Delaware, recently tried informally to quantify just how enthusiastic modern Europeans are for North American plants. He analyzed a stack of current catalogues from European nurseries and found that nearly one-fourth of the plants offered were North American natives. The catalogue selections included everything from goldenrods to sunflowers to prairie plants, some of which have lately found their way into U.S. gardens. They also offered a lot of the woodland plants that have been ignored by American gardeners—and the nurseries where they shop.

To help build interest in native plants, the plants' aficionados have employed a number of tactics. Some, like Joni Janecki, have simply begun using the plants more in the landscapes they design. Others have founded or joined organizations that advocate native plants, both by calling for their protection in the wild and by encouraging gardeners to use them in their gardens. (The groups do not encourage gardeners to take plants from the wild, but, rather, to buy natives that have been grown from seeds or cuttings.) The New England Wildflower Society, founded in 1900, is the oldest and best known of these organizations. Former first lady Lady Bird Johnson has helped increase interest in native plants by establishing the National Wildflower Research Center, an institution devoted to studying and protecting them.

Finally, some have turned to legislation or regulations favoring native plants in created landscapes. Most of these efforts have been at the city and county level and have failed. One variation that succeeded, though, has had a nationwide impact.

During his first term, President Bill Clinton weighed in with a directive designed to make created landscapes on federal property more environmentally friendly. It followed recommendations initiated by Vice President Al Gore to figure ways to run a more efficient, cost-conscious government. The directive instructed federal agencies to use native plants in their landscapes as much as possible. The idea was to create landscapes that reflect the region and that rely on plants naturally adapted to the local climate.

The nursery industry as a whole blasted the directive. It argued that the order was unreasonable and discriminated against widely available and attractive exotic plants. The industry felt many of its members' businesses, based on acres of hardy, adaptable exotics, would suffer. In contrast, the American Society of Landscape Architects lauded the directive for its regional and environmental sensitivity. The organization saw it as a small step toward doing what many landscape architects had advocated for generations. It took ecology into account as well as regional landscape distinctions. After weighing the comments, the White House stood firm and made the order official. Native plants would get a place in the federal garden. But the directive added fuel to an already vocal backlash against native-plant talk.

The loudest and most widely heard voice in the backlash came from garden writer Michael Pollan in a 1994 *New York Times Magazine* article headlined "Against Nativism." In it, Pollan implied that recent native-plant enthusiasm is part of a general anti-immigrant fervor sweeping America. He noted that research by two landscape scholars has recorded unquestionable links between Nazism and a native-plant fervor in late-1930s Germany. Pollan also suggested that in America today people who advocate natural-looking gardens and native plants are bullying the rest of the gardening world into following their lead.

Months after Pollan's article was published, native-plant proponents across the United States were still stinging from the piece. They responded in essays in newsletters and journals, including at least one academic journal for ecological restoration experts, and at conferences. Advocating that native plants be given a chance to compete for space in the created landscape, they said, shouldn't be confused with the kind of distasteful nativism directed at humans that Pollan talks about. One is about ecology and plants. The other is about bigotry toward people. "The first rule of statistics is that correlation doth not imply causation. Because you had Nazis gardening with native plants in the 1930s and you have tree huggers gardening with native plants in the 1990s does not mean the tree huggers are Nazis," ecologist and native-plant grower Neil Diboll told one audience.

In addition, some native-plant proponents maintained, most native-plant advocates do not demand that only native plants be allowed in the garden, or that only free-flowing natural designs be permitted. "Fringe loonies aside—and every organization, philosophy and movement attracts them—the countless people I know from all over the country who are drawn to the natural gardening approach are as tyrannical as Santa Claus," garden writer and native-plant gardening guru Andy Wasowski wrote in one response.

A full year after the Pollan article, the Brooklyn Botanic Garden opened a day-long symposium on native plants with what was billed as a debate between one of the scholars Pollan's piece referred to, landscape architect Joachim Wolschke-Bulmahn, and Diboll, a leading advocate of prairie restoration. The event was less debate and more gentle discussion between like-minded gentlemen, both passionately opposed to nativism and racism and their ugly rhetoric.

Yet the discussion highlighted a core difference that distinguishes contemporary native-plant advocates from the rest of gardening culture. The difference has nothing to do with how people view each other and everything to do with how they view the created landscape and its relationship to the wildlands.

Mainstream gardening culture views the created landscape as necessarily separate and different from the local wildlands. The created landscape is a place for humans to express their own tastes and interests, unrestrained by factors that shape natural plant communities.

"Many good reasons are being offered for the use of so-called native plants in gardens and landscapes, including low maintenance, adaptation to a place, preservation of wildlife and plants from extinction, aesthetic reasons, and others," Wolschke-Bulmahn told the Brooklyn audience. "But for me there is no reason for native-plant doctrine and for the assumption that only native plants would serve the above-mentioned purposes best . . . I do not see any reason why gardeners in, for example, Germany who may be intrigued by the wonderful illustrations in Neil Diboll's Prairie Nursery catalogue should not try to have a glimmer of the beauty of the American prairie reflected in their gardens."

In contrast, the native-plant proponents usually view the created landscape and the garden as a potential extension of wildlands, in spirit if not in fact. "What I see happening is a change from a more human-centered garden to a more meeting-nature-part-way type of garden. I think the motivation for the change in the relationship between humans and the gardens is predicated on the interconnectedness of all life," Diboll told the Brooklyn audience as he explained the thinking behind native-plant enthusiasm in America today. "And as we have literally destroyed the native habitats and ecosystems of North America, we're reflecting on what we've done. In this headlong rush to civilize the wilderness, suddenly we've civilized almost everything and we look back and say, 'Oh my goodness, perhaps we've gone too far.' "

XI

JONI STANDS BEFORE AN ATTENTIVE AUDIENCE OF fifteen men and one woman gathered around a U-shaped arrangement of faux-wood-topped tables. She gestures at the newest of three landscape design plans hanging on the conference-room wall behind her. "Again, we're looking at resurrecting nature, trying to reuse as much as we can," she explains. The audience sits motionless, giving no hint of either warmth or rejection. So far, so good.

This is the third time Joni has formally presented her firm's proposal for the asphalt desert in front of Hewlett-Packard's oldest trio of buildings. The first time, she won the bid to do the project. The second time, she showed a slightly more detailed plan to this same group, consisting of what HP insiders refer to as the project's customers. At that second presentation, Joni solicited suggestions about additions to her landscape plan. Smaller meetings with the project's management team, including Kevin Alford and Phil Koenig, followed. Now, with the most detailed version of the plan, she has returned to the customers for their critique.

Horror stories about landscape-plan presentations to corporate clients abound and Joni has heard many of them. There are the clients who hate everything, complain loudly, and demand changes on the spot. There are the clients who listen passively and shrug, offering no comments, good or bad. So far, Joni has been lucky. She has never been subjected to such horrors herself, but she went into this meeting equipped with the kind of small precautions that help guard against a change in luck. She was up late the night before, reviewing notes for her presentation. This morning she agonized over what to wear, finally settling on dressy but comfortable black slacks and a green-and-black silk shell. Then she left Santa Cruz earlier than necessary, so she would arrive at HP's Palo Alto headquarters without feeling frazzled and rushed.

Joni knows from chats with the project's management team that there is a second discreet agenda for this meeting, and it involves money, the mother of all headaches. Many of the suggestions the customers have proposed since she first began her design have added unknown dollars to the project's cost. The customers mainly represent two company divisions, ICBD, whose move to the site prompted the landscape planning in the first place, and HP Labs. A third division, Corporate, is responsible for picking up the tab. If the customers like the expanded plan enough—and want it enough—the project's managers are hoping HP Labs will pony up some additional cash. Joni's job, then, is to explain her new plan, subtly selling its newest features to HP Labs, while alerting the group that what they want is going to take more money than the $400,000 the Corporate Division has allotted.

"This is where we were when we last met, and several things came up," she continues as she runs through the plan's basic layout. To an outsider, it might look like an abstract drawing. Three rectangles balance on their corners atop a mosaic of curvy lines, columns, and ameboid shapes. The shapes are symbolic representations. Rectangles are buildings, curvy lines and columns equal paths and borders, ameboid shapes are trees and plant groups. Joni reminds the group that three courtyards fill the angles where the buildings meet—Cougar Den, Deer Court, Acorn Court. Then she highlights some of the new additions. Falcon Roost, an expansion of an existing group picnic area, will add more landscape to another side of Building 2. HP Labs occupies Building 2. Acorn Court, tucked in the elbow of Buildings 4 and 6, will be home to a new water feature. It won't be the typical corporate landscape fountain with water streams jetting skyward like a mini-version of Old Faithful. This will be subtler, calmer, more like something that might be found in California's backcountry. It will look like a giant boulder, marked with the kind of smooth round impressions indigenous people would make while grinding acorns. A gentle stream will trickle across the boulder and into a pool barely bigger around than a birdbath.

"There are a variety of choices in pathways," she tells the group. An existing walkway hugs the building, and an inner walkway traverses the courtyards, where "you feel like you're in the habitat." And then there are the pathways that lead out to the parking lot and beyond. Graphically, all the courtyards and pathways look similar on paper, Joni indicates. In reality, she intends to distinguish one from the other by using different plants. Deer Court, for instance, will include dense pockets of deer grass, a tall grass that grows in thick bunches, where deer like to browse and lie.

The customers listen. Occasionally someone asks a question. "Are you considering that in the wintertime the shadows extend . . ." a man begins. "Out to here . . ." Joni picks up, pointing to a spot beyond the edge of a courtyard.

Talk turns to lighting. "We've tried to match the existing lighting situation as much as possible," she explains. She is still contemplating whether to add pathway lights to supplement the beams cast by the existing overhead lights dotting the parking lot.

"I wouldn't want to walk out there without lights," one man says.

"You'd have to worry about a cougar getting you," a wag adds, prompting a ripple of laughter.

Joni winds up her explanation of the plan and looks to the group. At first with the speed of thick syrup, then gradually faster, the comments roll forward. An engineer compliments her on the water feature. Another remarks that the pathway to Building 6 needs to be strong enough to withstand the weight of heavy forklifts. That means extra cement and extra labor. Joni looks at Steve Shokrai, whose job it will be to persuade the money managers to add to the funding pot. She makes a thumbs-up and mouths "Big bucks."

The group's concerns turn to what should be dropped to cut costs, and different voices chime in with advice. Cut the small bus-stop shelter at the end of the parking lot, someone suggests. Not that, snaps back one man who commutes by bus. So what should go? Someone suggests using smaller plants. Soon comments veer off to areas outside Joni's plan.

Remove the oleanders that line the end of the parking lot, one man demands. Can't be done, someone else observes. It would expose the view of the parking lot to Building 20, the main administration building. With a diplomat's smoothness, Steve interrupts and recommends holding off specific cost-cutting advice until the whole estimate comes in, "and then see what to drop or whether to go for more money."

Finally, a representative from HP Labs remarks that the revised plan is more balanced across the site, giving almost equal weight to courtyards in front of each of the three buildings. He likes it, he says. For a precious moment, further funds seem a distinct possibility. Then, he adds, "I don't want to see [the balance] disappear when you have to cut costs."

The discussion drags to a stop and the meeting ends. Joni has spent an hour with the group, most of it fielding questions. As people trail out of the room, Steve congratulates Joni on a job well done, then slips out of the room, leaving her to talk technical details with Kevin, Phil, and the project's contractor, hired only a few weeks earlier, Bob Benson.

Later, over lunch at a downtown Palo Alto restaurant, Joni beams about the good response. Nobody yelled, nobody complained, nobody charged to the front and drew on her plans to illustrate a point. "They really liked them! I mean, I never thought they'd like the ideas the way they like them," she says between bites of Guatemalan beans and rice. "They're just so into it. They use the names when they talk about it. To me that's like . . . they identify with it. They can talk about Bear Paw and Deer Court and Cougar Den."

But her enthusiasm is muted by that one big worry, the

budget. The landscape will cover just under one and a half acres, nearly an acre of which will be plantings. Now the area is covered with asphalt and concrete, much of which will have to be removed. Tearing up and then hauling away and dumping that heavy waste is going to be expensive—much more expensive, Joni now realizes, than she originally figured. When she put together her first estimate, she figured the bill for demolition and dumping would be only a fraction of what she now believes might mount to at least $100,000. She fears that, with the addition of Falcon Roost and other elements the customers have requested, the whole project cost might reach $1 million. That's more than twice what HP originally said it wanted to spend, and twice as much as Joni estimated her first version of the plan would cost. "That's just a guess," she says gloomily. "I hope I'm overreacting."

What can you say about thousands of square feet of old asphalt? It's thick, it's heavy, it smells, and it's dusty. It's also one big expense Joni can't avoid. On this job, it comes attached in some cases to old concrete sidewalks and curbs that have to be removed. If it were a smaller job, with only a bit of concrete, Joni might consider using some of it in the landscape. She could, for instance, use broken concrete as a base for the mounds of dirt that workers will shape into sinuous berms before planting. Doing this would fit into her theme for the HP landscape of reuse and resurrect, and it would save money. But there will be too much demolished concrete to hide beneath dirt on this site, and asphalt has an annoying tendency to soften when it gets warm, making it unstable for a mound base. So Joni has to settle for what is becoming an increasingly common destination for old asphalt and concrete: the recycling plant.

On a barren hilltop a dozen miles from HP's Palo Alto headquarters sits a second, more unusual hill. This one is about three stories high and as wide as a city block. It is a vision of black-and-white rubble. From behind sunglasses, John Armando gazes at the hill. "This entire mountain is asphalt and concrete," he exclaims with the fast-clipped chatter of a salesman. There are bench-size pieces of concrete torn away from dying buildings, and table-size chunks of asphalt evicted from parking lots. And there is the odd porcelain toilet or two thrown into the mix.

The mountain belongs to Raisch Products, a company that recycles construction and demolition debris. On any given day, the mountain swells as trucks dragging trailers filled with asphalt, concrete, and porcelain rumble up the hill and dump their holdings. Then the mountain shrinks as stray lumber and metal are sorted out and a crane swoops down like the starring dinosaur in an old Japanese monster movie to grab mouthfuls of the remaining debris.

The crane stops short of chewing the stuff and instead spits it into a giant container locked to a line of shutes and conveyor belts that move high aboveground not far from the debris mountain. At points along the route, the contents are mechanically smashed and sorted, smashed and sorted, over and over until all that is left is a bin of stray metal and a black alp of pulverized concrete and asphalt.

Armando, the company's recycling manager, stabs a one-foot-by-one-foot section of asphalt with his finger. "This will go through the crusher like butter," he purrs above the mechanical cacophony. He points to another pile of clean concrete, each piece the size of a football. "This is what we call cherry; this is beautiful." It has no metal rods of reinforcement (called rebar) to sort out, no wooden supports—it's pure concrete.

Somedays as many as a hundred trucks carrying eighteen to twenty tons each dump here. It is up to ten times cheaper per load to dump here than at a conventional landfill. And what is dumped here eventually returns to work. Contractors—sometimes the same ones who brought the raw debris—buy the black mountain of pulverized material to use as the base aggregate for new roads and parking lots. By its tenth year in the business, Raisch had recycled enough asphalt and concrete to build a thick road from San Francisco to San Diego. "That's enough material to fill Candlestick Park to the brim," Armando says. Raisch is just one of many companies beginning to benefit from a national trend toward landfill alternatives.

In the pre-enlightened days of old, it was simple guiltlessly to dig up unwanted asphalt, load it by the dozerfull into a dump truck, and haul it away to become one with a stadium-size hole in the ground. The costs included trucking and relatively cheap landfill dumping fees. Now people realize that landfills are not endless and garbage out of sight is never permanently out of the way. Wastes, including construction wastes, are not benign. Their problems are varied. They can leach toxins into aquifers or just take up space that would otherwise feature something more pleasant and desirable. So states, counties, and cities have taken measures to reduce waste by raising dump fees and creating laws to encourage recycling. There's nothing like a high dump fee to make recycling tantalizing.

Only a generation or two ago, landscape architects rarely thought twice about where the hardscape they ordered would end up when it was ready to be replaced. Nobody really cared if concrete or asphalt would have to be recycled. Now Joni and many of her contemporaries take that into consideration, and not just to save money down the road. They are trying to practice "sustainable" landscape architecture, something they figure will be more gentle on the environment.

Sustainable landscape architecture—the term, the idea, and how to put it into practice—is still evolving. Its foundation rests partly in a book published in 1969, a year before the first Earth Day, and well before the term "sustainable" became such a common adjective in environmental discussions. The book is Ian McHarg's *Design with Nature*. In it, McHarg, a landscape architect and educator, calls on other landscape architects to be more sensitive to the natural environment—its contours, its waterways, its ecology—as they design, particularly as they draft regional and community plans. The book suggests a radical departure from the bulldozer-driven, large-scale landscapes that mushroomed across America after World War II.

Twenty-six years later, another landscape architect, Robert L. Thayer, Jr., took landscape architects a step further down the road of environmental sensitivity. He took them into the world of sustainability. Other landscape architects have written and talked about sustainability, but with his book, *Gray World, Green Heart*, Thayer gave what may be the most influential explanation of the term and how to apply it.

He defines a sustainable landscape as "a physical place where human communities, resource uses, and carrying capacities of surrounding ecosystems can all be perpetually maintained." And he provides a list of general characteristics that all sustainable landscapes have. Sustainable landscapes aren't energy hogs, mostly relying on renewable energy sources. They "maximize the recycling of resources" and produce little waste. They don't rock the balance of the surrounding ecosystem. They help the people who live in and around them. Finally, in sustainable landscapes, "technology is secondary and subservient, not primary and dominating."

It is harder to create a sustainable landscape than a conventional landscape. You have to think about the source and impact of everything at each step. It is much easier simply to lay a lawn, plant pretty shrubs, build a big fountain, and wire in high-energy lights without thinking about plant biodiversity, wildlife value, water and energy conservation. But the long-term benefit of the extra thought, according to sustainability advocates like Thayer, is a better quality of life for the people who live in those landscapes. The plants will regenerate on their own. The landscapes will last in harmony with the natural world and with people.

Most created landscapes in America, especially large-scale landscapes, are riddled with the kind of hardscape details and technological dependence that make them hostile partners with nature. Wooden benches, stone or concrete pots, metal grates, electrical lighting, cement pathways, and plastic irrigation piping all are made at some cost to the environment. We mine the earth, cut forests, build power plants, and burn fossil fuels to create hardscape.

Some of the hardscape is mostly cosmetic. Fountains, for example, are rarely essential. Some details, such as grates that rest over tree wells, are utilitarian and make landscape maintenance more convenient. Some are essential to keep alive softscape that hasn't been selected with sustainability in mind. For instance, certain plants, and that includes picture-perfect grass in lawns, fall apart without regular watering; hence the demand for sprinkler systems in arid climates. Or they don't thrive without chemical fertilizers. Or they aren't adapted to fight the local pests, so they succumb to everything from fungi to mites unless they are routinely shellacked with pesticides.

But even those people who philosophically resist this kind of techno-dependence can't get away from it entirely. People are constantly confronted by the dual gods of Technology and Nature fighting for space in the landscape, Thayer notes. "Most Americans must subconsciously practice acceptance of the nature-technology inconsistency every day of their lives, lest they be driven crazy by an overwhelmingly ambivalent landscape." Landscape architects are subjected to a steady stream of advertising from bench makers, lighting makers, stoneware dealers. Get yourself on a garden magazine's mailing list, and in no time you, too, will find your mailbox packed with catalogues from companies peddling tools and hardscaping to add to your garden.

Joni likes the idea of sustainable landscaping. But she lives in the real world of clients for whom the simple act of ordering up a design that includes native plants can be a radical step. She makes compromises between what she thinks is the *best* thing from an environmental perspective and what it is *possible* to do.

She addresses sustainability in the softscapes she designs by choosing plants that are naturally suited to the local climate, won't demand a lot of fertilizers or pesticides, and have a chance of regenerating over time. She addresses sustainability in the hardscapes she designs by trying to reduce their impact. She tries to tear out less, recycle more, and limit the environmental damage caused by the new things she puts in. She prods her clients into considering benches made from recycled plastics instead of freshly timbered and milled wood. She considers where decorative boulders and stonework come from and avoids including them, or she looks for ways to lessen the environmental damage that including them might cause. Sometimes it takes creative thinking to reduce the impact of hardscape. It may require turning to non-natural sources to protect nature. It may even require help from a man who makes dinosaurs.

The path to the dinosaur maker is about as winding and only slightly less direct than the route to Oz. It begins when Joni assigns intern Jack Kiesel, a landscape-architecture student, the task of planning a field trip. The Janecki & Associates staff will take a day off from computers and drafting tables to tour significant landscapes. It will be fun, educational, and maybe, Joni hopes, boost what she fears is a dip in office morale.

Jack takes to field-trip planning like a travel agent to cruise-line schedules. He combs old magazines to come up with a list of significant landscapes, the kind that have won national competitions and received rave reviews from the profession's stars. He pieces together an itinerary and prepares road maps. The route will loop through San Jose and up to Berkeley, then back again, with frequent stops along the way. Come trip day, Joni, Robin, Michael, and Jack meet at the office at 9 a.m., then pile into Joni's Subaru station wagon, like big kids ready for adventure.

In San Jose, they visit a large urban park built along a channeled river. Michael and Jack sketch stairways and railings and general scenes. Robin writes in a notebook. Joni examines the mixed use of some currently popular California natives along the river corridor, and wonders aloud why some trees are planted so close together. In another part of town, they visit a tiny renovated park that features a central walkway lined by shade trees and benches. Then they drive to a reclaimed waste dump that has been transformed into a walking and jogging park on the edge of a marsh. Jack and Joni seem enchanted by the crushed seashell the designer used on the pathways. Joni notes that the planted native grasses throughout the landscape have been overcome by weeds. She would have specified more maintanence, she remarks later.

At one stop Joni planned herself, the designers find something entirely unexpected: a dinosaur skeleton half-buried in sand at the shallow, sloping beach end of a back-yard swimming pool. Only it isn't *really* a skeleton and it isn't *really* sand. The bony sunbather is a cement replica, and so is the sand. The four designers stand around the pool for a moment, analyzing it. They touch the skeleton. They bend close to examine the way the pool's phony beach has been painted to resemble the real thing. Robin throws her sandals off and wades in a few inches. One by one, the others remove their shoes, while Joni walks up a pathway leading to a rise above the boulder-circled pool.

The boulders run from big to huge and are arranged to suggest a backcountry watering hole tucked into a rocky hill, rather than a swimming pool in a suburban back yard. It looks like a thoughtless soul—maybe even a landscape architect—dismantled a beautiful wilderness scene, stole the rocky furniture right out of some rattlesnake's front yard. The truth is that these boulders are no more authentic than the dinosaur. They are stones cast from cement and fiberglass and painted to mimic a real boulder's appearance.

Joni added this side trip so she could get a firsthand look at the boulders. The yard belongs to Matt Wilson, the dinosaur and boulder maker himself. Joni wants HP to contract him to create the boulder fountain. Now, as she sees the range of his rock work, she thinks she might have more for him to do.

Joni has planned to spread a few large boulders across the HP landscape. Next to plants, boulders are probably the oldest landscape accent. Before there were bronze statues, wooden benches, clay pots, or ceramic birdbaths, there were boulders. They provide a nice backdrop for grasses and flowering plants. They help vary the topography and add to the landscape's natural appearance. But they have drawbacks. They are heavy and hard to move. Their size and shape are random. And for Joni the most troubling problem is their origin. Boulders are like diamonds. They are attractive jewels in a landscape, a coveted accessory, but their costs exceed simple dollar value. It is virtually impossible to get boulders without leaving some kind of scar on the earth. Getting a boulder means taking one from someplace, creating a vacant spot, or digging a giant quarry.

Joni stomps her boot on one of the boulders. It feels firm, but there is a faint hint of a hollow sound. She knocks on a larger one. No echo. She is satisfied they pass the obvious sensory tests of sight, sound, and touch. These faux rocks look and feel real. Granted, they don't come without their own environmental problems. They are made from materials that require a lot of open-pit mining or waste-generating manufacturing. But to Joni, creating the cement rocks seems less environmentally offensive than stripping a local canyon or hauling in rocks from some distant natural spot. She makes a note to call the dinosaur maker to talk about boulders.

Not long after HP hired Joni to design its landscape, the company hired Bob Benson as the project's contractor. Benson, a tall man who favors polished cowboy boots and Western-style shirts, is responsible for building the landscape that Joni designs. His is mostly an office job. He spends his time finding the subcontractors—the asphalt demolishers, the cement pourers, the plant planters—and helping marshal the project through the city's building department for permits. And one of his first tasks is to estimate the project's construction costs.

One day in late March, about two weeks after Joni's presentation, Benson faxes his first estimates to Joni and the HP project managers. The price tag is astronomical. Benson estimates it will cost more than $1.2 million to resurrect nature. All the new additions—the extra courts, the back-country version of a water fountain—increase costs, but tearing out sidewalks and putting in new pathways jacks up the building cost much more than she first imagined. Even recycling wouldn't bring demolition under $100,000.

Steve Shokrai had expected Joni's expanded plan to come in over budget. He did not expect the costs to be so high, though. He and his team are simply shocked at first. "We all kind of got carried away with the beauty of the design," he says several days after seeing Benson's estimate. Nevertheless, Steve remains calm and methodically considers the options. There is still time, after all. Indeed, the team brought Benson in early so they could get estimates before the project was so far along that changes would be hard. The team knew that Joni's firm was young, and Steve notes that strict adherence to budgets is rare in young designers. "Those types of things you've got to learn by experience." Joni is asked to come to Palo Alto in a week with cost-cutting ideas.

Joni is back at the drawing board, spending part of a weekend alone in her office working out new approaches.

She wants to keep the plan's original spirit while reducing its scope, so she knows there is a limit to how much she will feel comfortable eliminating. "We really wanted to create meaningful larger areas that could be used for a discussion of not fragmenting the habitat," Joni explains. "But as soon as you start to squeeze it and isolate it, it becomes just a little space and it doesn't have as much meaning. Yeah, it's a nice little courtyard, but it doesn't connect with the rest of that area."

Her deadline is Wednesday. By Tuesday evening, she feels miserable, stricken by a head cold. "I don't know how to present this stuff," she says, groaning, as she reviews three ideas she has come up with. Early the next morning, she loads her canvas satchel into the back of her station wagon, then slides into the driver's seat to go the fifty miles to Palo Alto. She drives along Highway 17, a busy scenic roller-coaster road that scales the wooded mountains separating Santa Cruz from the rest of the state. She descends into the small cities and suburbs of Silicon Valley, disparate parts linked together by a web of freeways. She takes the freeway that leads to Palo Alto. Concrete sound walls, green treetops, tract homes, and occasionally signs for gas stations and office buildings fill the roadside view. As she approaches Palo Alto, the scenery becomes more open, greener, the houses more distinctive, the wealth more visible.

At HP, she finds herself at a round table amid a maze of partitions and desks. Phil Koenig and Ted Dukelow are already there. Kevin Alford has been promoted and Steve has made Ted the project's manager. Joni is a little worried about this shift. Kevin combined precise organization with open enthusiasm. He has been a valuable cheerleader for the project. Although Ted is friendly, his feelings about the project are harder to read. Joni wonders how the company dynamics will work now and whether she will have a strong backer, an advocate for the design.

Steve arrives and settles into a seat. He has been thinking about the project in the last few days, and before Joni can present her ideas, he proposes a solution. Speaking in quiet tones ornamented with a lyrical Persian accent, he says he doesn't want to lose the landscape's main ideas. He likes the plan as it is, so he suggests Joni simply scale back a little and prepare to phase it in over time. In the first phase, he suggests retaining Acorn Court and Salmon Run, the pathway across the parking lot. He also wants to make sure two other courtyards, Deer Court and Cougar Den, spanning the buildings occupied by HP Labs, get done as well. He needs to consult with his boss, but he thinks the Corporate Division will raise the budget by about $350,000 to get the first phase completed, although it looks unlikely that HP Labs will contribute any extra money.

It is as though Steve has read Joni's mind and picked from it the approach she hoped she would be able to convince the team to take. Clearly, the design still has an advocate. The landscape is back on track, and Joni is delighted. Another worry doll can return to its basket.

At some point in almost every landscape project—corporate, public, or residential—someone says or thinks: "If money were no object . . ." Money is one of the four features that stand as steady as steel walls in the way of perfect landscapes. The other three are time, taste, and client awareness. Landscape architects are constantly battling these four devils. But none is as confounding as money.

If money were no object, by the time the winter rains began to subside, Dennis and Abbe would be finished with the first phase of the design Joni created for their yard. Money is an object, though, and when they had to choose between putting in a new drain system to carry water away from the old house's foundation or putting in the landscape, the drain system won. It turned out to be a wise choice. The winter rains were fiercer than in many years, burying memories of a recent seven-year drought. Knee-high weeds, green as shamrocks, have sprouted where only a few months earlier there was nothing but dirt, and Abbe jokes that migratory ducks may be nesting among them.

Dennis decides to tend to the weeds when spring arrives and the rainy season has passed. He buys a mower and clips the tall grasses, mustard flower, and wild radish into a flowerless green mat that almost looks like a lawn. Until the spring and summer heat suck all moisture from the topsoil, the weed lawn is green. From their front door, they see the lawn and the Sands begin to want. Their thoughts, lately focused on drains and foundations, turn to landscape again. They want to block the unhindered view into their yard and house first, build the front wall, gate, and driveway.

"What we really need at this juncture is the privacy and to get our driveway together, to get some of the mud and dirt down," Abbe says in early spring. Confident because they've done their own contracting on house remodels, the Sands decide to be their own contractors on the landscape. They have started investigating what kind of surface they want and will spend part of the summer getting bids from suppliers and figuring out exactly what needs to be done and in what order. "We better have a good plan down before we end up doing things and have to tear them out. We hate to redo things," she says, with a laugh, "It's not a good look."

A few months later, the Sands are still exploring the best way to proceed. What sort of surface should they use on the driveway? What kind of fence should they put in? Will the driveway area need irrigation installed first? Doing the landscape is so much more complicated than it appears, Dennis explains, and the underlying work, like the grading and irrigation, costs a lot.

The Sands would execute the entire landscape plan in a minute if money were no object. But it is for them, just as it is for HP and its landscape face-lift; for Ed Piper and his park dream; for the reluctant gardener and the dog-trampled back-yard weed patch passing as lawn that really ought to be replaced.

"Our philosophy is, we're not going to borrow money to do any of this. So it's about saving it and doing it as we go along," Dennis says. "We're going very, very slowly because it's a matter of money."

XII

VISIT A COLLEGE OR UNIVERSITY LANDSCAPE-architecture program toward the end of any term and watch the students. They are giddy with exhaustion from pulling multiple all-nighters to meet a deadline for a design plan. They hunch over drafting tables and computers in studios that look like small warehouses partitioned into work spaces, sometimes working together, sometimes independently. All that matters is that they apply their new technical skills and creativity to solve a problem. They rarely have to consider an actual client's tastes or limited budget. They don't have to negotiate with a harried contractor twice their age about whether a slab of concrete has been laid according to plan. They spend precious little time in formal meetings. When they have finished their project, they get a sure appraisal.

Landscape-architecture students are like medical students, who can focus on medicine and ignore health-insurance forms. Instructors shield them from the profession's tedious and trying elements, figuring they'll learn enough about that on the job. Only later will the novice landscape architects realize that, despite the hellish hours and ridiculous deadlines, their student days were a profession's paradise.

In the world outside, landscape architects' lives are chockful of meetings—meetings with clients, meetings with subcontractors, meetings with contractors. This is a business that demands teamwork and compromise at almost every turn. The designer's creative vision and technical expertise struggle against a mountain of hurdles, including client whim. If a completed landscape looks anything like the architect's plan, it is because the landscape architect has been tirelessly persistent and endlessly persuasive—and has attended a lot of meetings.

Eight months into the Hewlett-Packard landscape project, and no ground has yet been broken. No asphalt has been removed, no trenches dug, no lights installed, no shrubs planted. Joni has attended a dozen meetings, but nothing about the sterile parking flat that hugs the company's first buildings has changed except on paper. And there, on paper, it changes over and over again as Joni and Michael slice and redraw their plans, peeling away a pathway here and a courtyard there.

"They're thinking about switching Deer Court to Cougar Den," Joni says one day in early June, groaning. The switch would mean reducing Deer Court's size and increasing Cougar's size. Cougar, she explains, is beside the building occupied by HP Labs, a division with clout and a burning desire for a nice landscape. But corporate politics alone aren't responsible for the latest design request. There is also a problem with truck deliveries. It seems that a plan to have cafeteria deliveries moved to the other side of one building, to keep trucks from interfering with the landscape, has fallen through. Joni will have to make sure there is room for large trucks to turn around beside Deer Court. In addition, walkways there will have to be reinforced to tolerate heavy equipment rolling in and out of the building.

The design changes mean more time at the drafting table, hours Joni hadn't counted on when she started the job. Already there have been more meetings, more long drives to Palo Alto, more time away from other work at the office, than she had anticipated when she set her fee for the project.

As a group, landscape architects have moderate salaries compared with many professions. Fees vary from one part of the country to another, but generally a principal like Joni in a small firm charges between $60 and $90 an hour. The rate for work done by young staffers is about $45. The rule of thumb is that a firm charges the client approximately three times what the firm is paying the designer. The idea is to charge enough to cover salary and overhead and still have something left over to grow with. With this in mind, Joni responds to the latest design request with a letter to HP explaining what the changes would entail—mainly, more billable work. She suggests an additional fee. "I think it's only fair," she says later, with uncharacteristic impatience. "I can't keep spending my time—they're not making up their friggin' minds."

Days later, Joni drives to Palo Alto for yet another meeting. This time she huddles with project manager Ted Dukelow and his boss, Steve Shokrai, about the new changes.

The two men agree the latest fee request is justified. Later, as they chat about the project, Steve predicts that her business will boom when the landscape is done. It will help put her on the map with landscape architecture's stars.

In November 1992, another HP landscape was featured among outstanding landscapes in *Landscape Architecture*, the profession's leading magazine. The design was one of a handful of honorable mentions awarded in the American Society of Landscape Architects' annual design contest. The contest's judges gave it glowing reviews. "It's a sculpture," the magazine quoted one judge. "Visually, it is a flowing, interconnecting system. It's just beautifully done," said another. Zen-like, spare in its execution, "evocative of a natural landscape, but it clearly isn't natural," chimed a third.

A nationally known San Francisco firm, whose reputation has since grown even greater, created the design. About three years later, the firm's principal was featured on the cover of the magazine. Winning an ASLA honor is to a landscape architect what winning a National Book Award is to a writer or winning the a National Spelling Bee is to a grade-schooler. It looks great on a résumé. Being featured on a *Landscape Architecture* cover is one of the ultimate signs of having arrived.

During a visit to the HP site one day, Joni and Michael wander over to see the famous landscape. It is surrounded by buildings, including a ground-floor cafeteria designed with a circular wall of windows. It is green and rolling. Serpentine concrete pathways wind through grassy berms. As *Landscape Architecture* described it: "A path angles across the landscape but disappears when it meets the mounds, encouraging workers to continue walking and explore the landscape. Groups of saw-cut rocks form benches that nestle into the landforms." It is a user-friendly landscape, the magazine reports.

On this day, during the lunch hour, the air is warm and the sun shines. Groupings of elm trees shade some areas. Yet every bench, every saw-cut rock, is empty. Behind the cafeteria window, diners are packed in tight, but nobody has carried a tray or brown bag out to enjoy the landscape. And that has become this landscape's biggest curiosity.

Some created landscapes are clearly not designed to encourage people to walk through or sit in them. Natural area restorations, for instance, are principally designed to help return ecological balance to a wild place. If people enjoy hiking through the area without destroying it, fine. But happy human interaction with the restored area is usually not the first thing a landscape architect has in mind for such a project. Some landscapes, though, are meant to be used. They invite people in to walk the pathways, touch the fountains, rest on the benches. Their architects want these landscapes to be alive with people. They design them to allow contemplation or to encourage socializing. Either way, the designers intend the landscapes to be more than just three-dimensional artwork admired from afar or in magazines.

This courtyard was designed to be used but rarely is. HP's Phil Koenig speculates that people avoid sitting in it because it is surrounded on all sides by buildings with windows. People sitting or strolling in this landscape see the windows and wonder if they are being watched. "I kind of agree with Phil," Joni says as she and Michael sit on one of the stone benches, their feet cushioned by thick turf. "I think people are like hamsters; they stay against the edges." They don't like to be in direct view. But there are some view obstructions in this courtyard. The berms rise up several feet, like small mountain ranges divided by the winding river of concrete sidewalk.

Michael wonders about the spare, built-in concrete seats that discreetly invite visitors to stay. He measures their height with a tape measure and decides they are a standard, acceptable height, neither too tall nor too short. The two designers walk along the path and stop to examine the turf. It is soggy in the lower areas, drier atop the berms. Water must roll down the berms. These grassy hills remind Joni of a Los Angeles architect who likes to incorporate steep sod edges into his designs. "He's always trying to push how far a lawnmower can go," she says.

Seeing this landscape go unused gets Joni thinking about her project. She and Michael have designed the animal courts to encourage workers to be in nature during their breaks. While designers want the new landscape to look attractive from the buildings, they clearly want it to be used. They want people to sit in it, to stroll the paths and admire the plants, to spend time beside the soothing mountain spring flowing over rocks. Maybe, she suggests to Michael, they need to organize field trips into their created habitats after the landscape is done. They need to explain to people how they've created the landscape, why they've made it the way they have. Maybe they just need to invite the engineers and computer wizards to enjoy nature.

Landscape architects may divide a landscape project into several stages. There is the first stage, during which the client is wooed, followed by the stage in which design concepts are developed. There is another when fine plans are made, and a fourth during which those plans are translated into necessary construction documents. Late in the process, but before construction begins, there is a period for selecting materials, making plant lists, bringing in lighting and irrigation experts, and seeing the plan through a maze of local permit requirements. When things aren't going just right, each stage can feel like a hurdle that can't be overcome. But when the process is smooth, each step can be plain fun.

Paring a landcape design to match a budget is not entertaining, but once it is done the fun begins. What seemed slow and impossible suddenly speeds up and every move is forward and concrete—sometimes, literally concrete. The kernel of an idea that started so many months ago—in this case, to introduce nature to an asphalt plain—actually begins to take shape in three dimensions. The landscape architect's work becomes more varied. The designer spends less time alone with a drafting table—or, in some especially modern practices, a computer loaded with design software. There is more time on site, helping translate the paper design into a landscape that will be a daily part of thousands of lives.

By early August, Joni and Michael are buoyant as they

arrive at HP to talk plants, furniture, and colored concrete with Ted and Phil. Joni has spent part of a weekend compiling lists of plants that will create the landscape's different habitats. She has marked pages in a large plant book filled with photos of native and drought-tolerant plants so she can point to visual examples for Ted and Phil. Michael carries a box of colored concrete samples the size of playing cards and a poster-size piece of foam core he has decorated with photos of benches, trash bins, light poles, and bike racks. Feeling well prepared and confident, they wind through a maze of chest-high partitions and settle around a table with Phil and Ted.

Landscape architects collect three-ring binders the way other people collect photo albums, filling them with pictures and descriptions of trash bins and park furniture. Virtually every advertisement in *Landscape Architecture* offers to send product information. With a single postcard, a landscape architect can have a mailbox stuffed with information on copper-roofed gazebos, blue concrete, bronze herons, and polypropylene pond liners (safe for fish and aquatic plants). On a shelf in Joni's office, product binders vie for space with samples of interlocking concrete pavers and tiles made from recycled milk bottles. When the time comes to pick out furniture and lampposts for a new landscape, these binders are like a portable home-shopping network. Their innards provide the clip art landscape architects use to aid clients in their selection of decorative and functional hardscape that can unify a landscape.

As the meeting begins, Joni launches into a discussion of bike racks. Transportation needs have a huge effect on how landscapes are shaped. There have to be places for people to park their vehicles, whether bikes or cars or trucks. There have to be turnarounds to get delivery trucks in and out. In some landscapes, there have to be places for hotdog skateboarders to ride away from crowded urban sidewalks. And there have to be paths for people to walk.

One challenge landscape architects face is figuring out how to incorporate multiple transportation requirements without making a landscape look as if its primary purpose is to serve wheeled machines rather than people. In a culture that thrives on easy mobility, this is not always possible, even in places where logic suggests cars don't belong. Yosemite, Yellowstone, and Grand Canyon national parks, all noted for their dramatic natural landscapes, are burdened by too many cars and too little parking, especially during peak summer-vacation months. Despite bus-shuttle services and limits on numbers of visitors, cars seem to outnumber squirrels, bears, and birds. All a landscape architect can do there is build wooden screens and plant strategically placed shrubs to hide parking lots so the rumbling monsters are less visible.

Making room for bike parking is relatively simple. Making room for cars and trucks without clouding a landscape's natural intent is harder. At HP, Joni has few options for diminishing the feeling that cars and trucks are everywhere. The landscape is, after all, right next to a parking lot on land that had been part of that lot. But a few design tricks do help. Joni's plan calls for construction workers to grade the flat plain to include sinuous berms, and the foliage-covered hillocks will break the view of the parking lot for workers inside the buildings. On one seldom-used but necessary path for service trucks, Joni calls for grasses to be planted in a sunken honeycomb of blocks. The intention is to make a path that will look more like a greenway and less like a driveway.

Phil, normally the leader in these meetings, seems distracted. He flips through photocopy pages about materials and products that Joni distributed, while Ted questions the need for new bike racks. "You know this is going to add money to the project, and if they aren't fully utilized . . ." he says.

There are already a couple of bike lockers on the site. At an earlier customer meeting, one participant complained that the reserved locker spaces were in great demand and hard to get, so there ought to be additional racks. But Joni decides not to press for more racks now. This is the client's call. Besides, she figures, HP can install bike racks later if it wants.

Plants will give this landscape the best chance of distracting people from the motor herds parked beside it. Plants will be the one natural element in this picture, and how they are arranged will dictate its feel. And though the project's managers at HP are aware that Joni intends to use mostly natives, she knows as she begins her plant-list discussion at this meeting with Ted and Phil that she may face some resistance. Native-grass experiments on other parts of the HP campus have caused Phil headaches in the past. She figures he will try to avoid anything that he thinks might create similar problems in the future.

Joni pins a copy of the latest plan for the landscape on the partition beside the table and points to the abstract-looking designs that stand for the landscape in front of Building 2, now called Cougar Court and Cougar Den. "That area is intended to be more of an oak savanna with an open feeling, low overhead canopy trees, and nice spaces between the canopy and the lower story," she says. She points to a photo of a natural oak savanna she has brought along. "That's the image we see, where you have flowering perennials and then masses of shrubs with oaks above." To get there, she wants to keep a few sycamores already on the site, add oaks, and move an existing Chinese pistache tree and some ornamental pear trees.

"Is that a problem? Relocating trees that size?" Ted asks.

Phil assures him it won't be a problem as long as the move is made while the trees are in their dormancy.

In front of them, each of the men has several pages of plant lists, one for each court. There are native sedges and grasses, sagebrush and phlox, California fescue and bush anemone. There are also African sumac and Australian willows. These trees have already been used successfully on adjacent parts of the HP site and Joni figures they will blend with the natives she plans and help tie the new landscape to the old. Most of the plants are familiar to Phil, but Ted, whose specialty is electrical lighting, knows little about them. Joni offers to go through the lists and explain each plant's characteristics. This will be her only chance to talk to both men in detail about the plant selection, and she wants to make sure they understand what they will see once the planting is done.

"I don't know if Ted wants to go through them all," Phil says with an edge of impatience.

"No," Ted agrees, "just as long as I get the concept."

Joni shows no sign of disappointment and carries on with an overview of the planting plan. She points out highlights that will help vary the landscape's height, including some redwoods.

"You've changed some of the species of grasses in the meadow," Phil says as he flips through the plant list. He has such mixed feelings about native grasses that he sounds almost as if he is arguing with himself. "It's a political football with people right now. I'm having a lot of problems with the Stipa purpa—they want to know why we're not taking care of it, you know. It goes dormant in the summertime and just looks bad. I have to be careful, I don't want another mistake."

Joni holds firm on her meadow mix. "I think it's fine. We're not treading on totally new ground," she says. In some parts, the meadows will be dominated by yarrow, a lacy-leafed plant that will bloom flower heads if allowed to grow but will give a turf effect if mowed every few months. In others, there will be mixtures of native grasses, lupine, and sedges. To keep most of the native grasses looking fresh year after year, and to remove dead blades, the garden crew will have to cut them back hard every year or two. But they will regenerate quickly, and some will grow larger than others. The seed stalks of the native deer grass planned for parts of Deer Court will reach four feet high, while some of the meadow grasses will grow barely shin-high.

Since the early 1980s, free-flowing grasses that grow into

substantial plants with interesting seedy plumes have become almost mandatory in trendy gardens. These aren't the grasses turf is made of, but the grasses that grow into distinguishable plants, even when placed side by side. But the ornamental grasses most often seen in landscapes and found in nurseries in the United States are exotic plants unrelated to local plant communities. A couple of these exotic ornamentals, because of their ability to spread their seed and replant themselves, have become pesky weeds that take root in disturbed soil along roadways and then spread into adjacent wildlands. Native grasses are less widely used in landscapes, generally. However, some landscape architects and gardeners scattered around the country, including the grass-conscious Prairie states, have been able to play off the general ornamental-grass interest to promote native grasses. In a way, then, the exotic ornamental-grass fashion has helped open the gate for native grasses.

Phil begins to feel reassured as he hears Joni's grass plan. He appreciates that her meadow mix includes several different species, including buffalo grass, a Western native that some horticulturists promote for turf mixes. Not all the grasses will reach dormancy at the same time, an important point to Phil. In other native-grass plantings on the HP site, patches were planted with a single species of grass and everything in those patches hits dormancy simultaneously. A whole landscape suddenly shifts from green to brown. "So either it looks great or it looks like s-h-i-t," Phil says.

Without having to elaborate on her mixed-species plan, Joni listens as Phil explains it to Ted. "With a polyspecies situation, or whatever you want to call it, if one thing's not looking good, something else might be," he says. The concept is like that typically used for perennial gardens or flower beds. Gardeners plant a mix to ensure that something is always blooming. There is always an attractive display even after one variety or species has completed its flowering.

Ted seems satisfied with Phil's explanation and moves the conversation to trees. How big will the oaks be when they are planted, he asks. Joni has specified 15-gallon and 24-inch boxed trees, which refers to the kind of container the young plants will be delivered in. They will be about six feet tall, with trunks much thinner than a fence post. It will be several years before they create a canopied woodland.

Plant size is a difficult issue. Clients usually want newly created landscapes to look beautiful and finished the minute the last brick is laid and the last plant is planted. Finished for many people means the new landscape should look like something that just stepped out of a *House and Garden* photo spread. They want trees to be tall, shrubs to be full, perennials to be in full bloom soon, if not immediately. But to get a mature-looking landscape right away, you have to install mature plants and place them close together to fill in blank spaces. If you use mature plants, the landscape will not last as long as a young-plant landscape, because most of the plants are already in middle age. Also, mature plants are often harder to get established. They suffer more than young plants from the shock and trauma of being put into a new space. Placing plants close together also almost guarantees that they will begin tangling and bumping into each other as they struggle for room to grow. Finally, and not insignificantly, the bigger the pot, the more a plant costs. As anyone who has ever bought a six-pack of young annuals knows, they are a better deal than four-inch potted annuals.

In an ideal world, according to native-plant grower Paul Kephart, people would buy and plant only seedlings. Seedlings have more root than shoot, and it is the roots that are most important in establishing a good footing for many years of happy growing. Kephart has planted 5-gallon oak trees and 15-gallon oak trees at the same time in a restoration landscape. Five years later, the smaller and the larger trees had all grown to the same size and were indistinguishable.

Joni understands that smaller plants are better. But she needs to make clients happy and help them see that their vision of paradise is at least on the horizon. She stops short of planting seedlings and orders up trees that are large enough to have more than a seedling's presence when they are planted. Then she assures anyone disappointed by the size of the less than mature tree or shrub that it will grow.

Phil checks the time. He has other meetings to attend. He asks if he can borrow the plant book whose pages Joni has color-coded, and promises to get back to her with any comments he may have about the plant choices. They chat about redwood trees and Joni makes a note about a new variety with silvery foliage that Phil would like to see in the landscape. Then Phil and Michael arrange to meet later in the day at Palo Alto's city hall to begin putting the plans through the weeks-long permit process.

"So, have a cup of coffee and think about it," Joni says about the planting plan as she hands over the book. She urges Phil to take a careful look at the plant list, because "some of them are new."

"I like it. I like the meadow better now than even the last one I saw," he responds cheerily.

"It's evolving," she says. "It might change a little bit, but it will only get better."

Phil and Ted wander off in separate directions. Joni falls back into a chair and lets out a great sigh. She feels deflated. The meeting was painless and, at about an hour, relatively short. But she worries that the men were too distracted to give the plant list the kind of attention it needs.

If anything is likely to disappoint clients when a new landscape is finished, it will be some plant or group of plants. A plant is usually the one thing they are least familiar with before a landscape is created, the one thing that is most likely to surprise them when the project is done. Joni came prepared for a longer, more detailed discussion to try to head off later disappointment or complaints. "We worked so hard," she moans.

Later, as Michael and Joni stride across the parking lot, wending their way through the rows of minivans and compact sedans, Joni mentions a brief conversation she had with Steve Shokrai when she stopped near his partitioned work space after the meeting. He was worried that native plants would require extra maintenance. She assured him that after the first year they won't require extraordinary care.

"I think he's been talking to Phil," she tells Michael.

"What do they want?" Michael asks, a little exasperated.

"Plastic plants," she dead-pans.

"Holographic plants! Virtual landscape!" he offers.

They chuckle and any shadows cast by the morning meeting float away.

Hard surfaces play a big and sometimes unplanned role in created landscapes. They are the clean, predictable places in the landscape where people can stroll or sit without dirtying themselves or crushing delicate plants. But if they don't lead to the right spot or offer respite at the right place, hard surfaces can do nothing more than highlight a landscape design's weaknesses. If a carefully planned sidewalk doesn't follow the most logical or inviting route, people will usually make their own tracks, leaving the sidewalks behind and creating dusty, rutted paths through plantings and lawns.

One often repeated—and possibly apocryphal—tale relates how a brilliant landscape architect who was asked to design a college campus did nothing to the design after the buildings had been set in place. He waited until students had been on the grounds for several months, then he put in sidewalks following the footpaths students had worn into the campus as they made their way around. Anything he planted in the spaces between the sidewalks remained untrampled and flourished since the sidewalks met the students' own routes.

Hard surfaces also introduce subtle environmental changes in a landscape. Concrete, brick, tile, and stone are the materials landscape architects typically use to create pathways, patios, and plazas. None of these is particularly porous. More water runs off these surfaces than seeps through to be soaked into the ground beneath. Runoff has become a problem in suburbs and cities as more and more natural landscape, whose soil and roots work like sponges to absorb seasonal rains, is covered with hard surfaces, including asphalt roads. Rivers and streams that once were large enough to carry away the annual runoff rise to overflowing. Add to this the problem of keeping free of debris the drainage pipes designed to route the runoff to the sea or river and you've got incipient floods.

One design strategy sustainable-landscape advocates promote is limiting hard surfaces and making those that do go into a landscape more porous. In practice, that means avoiding concrete altogether, setting brick or stone courtyards in sand, and avoiding concrete joints, or creating sidewalks of decomposed granite instead of more solid materials. The blessing and curse of these alternatives is that they are less permanent, less stable, less solid. They don't make long-lasting, smooth driveways for taxi traffic; they don't stay impeccably flat and level for decades. Weather and time reveal wrinkles, dips, and bumps. For corporate or public landscapes, where clients want to signal stability and permanence, these alternatives are a hard sell. Concrete will do the job for the courtyards at Hewlett-Packard.

By the time Joni and Michael finish planning the HP landscape, it includes a lot of hard surfaces. Some, like the pathway from the three-building complex across the parking lot, are new. But the wide sidewalks that hug the zigzag outline of the buildings were already there. Joni originally thought she would remove at least portions of the old sidewalks and bring plants closer to the building, closer to the folks inside looking out. She dumped that idea, though, to save money. The project would cost less to build, and involve less demolition, if she just left the old sidewalks and figured a way to blend them into the new landscape. Besides, the old walkways can do double duty as forklift paths for heavy cargo headed into the buildings.

This simple solution created a tricky problem. The sidewalks' old concrete had become marred and faded over the years. The concrete in the new walkways and courtyards would have to match the color of the old. Without a match—or something very close to it—the new landscape would look as if it had been carelessly tacked onto the old walkways. It would be the landscape equivalent of mixing bold plaids with garish stripes.

Matching concrete is a snap if you're just talking about the standard dolphin-gray stuff. But the old HP concrete isn't standard gray. Indeed, if you look around at created landscapes, it becomes clear that standard gray is not all that standard, having gone the way of white bedsheets. Colors, particularly the muted variety that are intended to meld with the surrounding architecture, are now common.

The HP site's concrete is an indefinite shade whose location on a color wheel would probably be somewhere between rose and mauve. Neither Joni nor her contacts at HP know exactly where that color came from, what concrete manufacturer created and named it. So, on the mild summer afternoon after the plant meeting, Michael and Joni huddle over a concrete stairway at HP with a small but heavy box of concrete samples in dozens of colors and shades. The two designers are set to find at least one sample whose color is acceptable.

Michael selects a few pieces of concrete from the box and

lays them one by one atop a stair step. Joni considers them with him and they reject several until Michael finds a near-match. He turns it over to read a label identifying its color. Joni teasingly balks at the name. "How can we use *San Diego* Buff?" she says, alluding to its geographic incompatibility with this Palo Alto site. They settle on two that come even closer to matching the existing concrete. They are labeled Adobe Tan and Coachella, named after one of the state's dusty farming valleys, far in place and spirit from this urban parking lot.

Since the first hairy human learned how to build a fire, people have been trying to bring light to landscapes after sunset. It's easy to understand why. The world is scary when all you can see are the vague outlines of gently swaying tree limbs, shrub carcasses, and flower heads, and your ears are filled with the sound of unseen insects rubbing their scrawny legs together in song. It's even scarier when you replace the garden scene with dark buildings, dark cars, dark parking lots, real crime threats, and a vivid imagination. Urban landscapes need light at night to ward off the criminally minded and to help keep everyone else from tripping over curbs and sidewalk cracks.

So there are good reasons to light landscape. To see how widely people agree on this, just consider the frequent introduction by nurseries and home-improvement stores of yet another garden light system that will simultaneously illuminate a garden's best features and protect valuable property. From fire-breathing tiki lanterns to solar-powered, mushroom-shaped Malibu lights, the home and garden industry continues to try to meet homeowners' primordial need for an outside night-light. None of the lights ever last long enough. Lanterns lose their wicks, and lawn lights get tipped by careless newspaper deliverers.

One afternoon, Joni arranges to meet a lighting consultant in the HP parking lot, and in just over half an hour he examines existing lights and wiring and sizes up the situation. Creating a lighting plan is part of the landscape architect's responsibility on a project like this. Like many small firms, Joni's typically subcontracts a lighting specialist to help plan and draft the construction documents that specify exactly where and what kind of electrical wiring has to be installed to accommodate adequate lighting.

Joni wants bollard lights at selected points along Salmon Run and in the courtyards. These lights usually rise two to three feet off the ground and look something like giant bullets. They are built to withstand kicking, bumping, and other abuse that would wipe out a tiki lantern. At about $750 apiece, they cost a small fortune, too. The eighteen the consultant recommends eat up the lighting budget for this phase of the landscape.

Joni would also like lights under some of the trees to illuminate them from below. There's no money for that now, though, so Joni decides instead to make sure enough electrical wiring is installed to make it possible to add them later. Even as she finalizes details for this scaled-back version of her firm's original landscape design, she clings to the promise of future phases. She wants to see the whole plan implemented someday.

XIII

A DEADLINE HANGS OVER THE HEWLETT-Packard project. Its funding is tied to a fiscal-year budget, which means that the design has to be done and construction ready to begin by October 31. When Joni began the project, that date was a comfortable year away. But now it is just weeks away, far too close. Last-minute details and unexpected problems keep demanding attention. Somedays it seems that nothing is working and the business of landscape architecture feels just about as fun as the life of a balloon at a porcupine's party.

Robin and Michael spend much of Labor Day weekend swapping long shifts on the computer to complete construction documents. The most detailed of the blueprints landscape architects create for any landscape, they are like X-rays that show exactly how a body's skeleton is put together. They detail dimensions and include instructions that direct the trench diggers, the asphalt cutters, the cement pourers, and the plant planters. Contractor Benson needs several copies right after Labor Day to pass out to subcontractors who are bidding on the project. To make sure it is getting the best work for the fairest price, HP wants Benson to collect bids from at least three different subcontractors in every specialty—three different demolition bids, three different concrete-construction bids, three different electrical-installation bids, and so on.

Meanwhile, the design wends its way through a mandatory review by outsiders. HP is located in the Stanford Research Park, which is owned and managed by Stanford University. The landscapes in the Stanford Research Park are an eclectic mix, dominated by the traditional corporate-park fare of exotic shrubs and the occasional expansive lawn. Before a company in the park can make any significant landscape changes, the plans have to be approved by the park's management company. Once the management company signs off on it, then the City of Palo Alto has to review the plans.

Stanford's review will be straightforward. The management company's landscape architect reviews the plans and decides if the new landscape is appropriate for the research park. It is primarily an aesthetic evaluation. The city's review will include aesthetic considerations, but it will also focus on technical details covered by various local ordinances, from parking requirements to water-conservation demands.

One morning, Joni, Michael, and Phil gather in a conference room at the Stanford Research Park's management company's offices. A large window spanning one wall looks out on an old oak tree that only barely survived a recent limb amputation. A tall metal crutch that seems to emphasize the tree's age helps support its surviving limbs. A formally clipped hedge of native manzanita frames the tree. It is a small picture of a native landscape done in a traditionally formal fashion. The view of the oak and the manzanita comforts the nervous trio as they wait to submit the landscape plan.

Michael holds a roll of blueprints and design drawings. Joni has brought along the boards bearing the sketches of the landscape that have helped win support for the project within HP. This is her first time through a review with this management company and she is prepared to make a formal presentation if necessary. But a serious young woman politely takes the blueprints, briefly examines them, and makes it clear no presentation is necessary. She asks a few questions about the documents and arranges for Michael to send her details about how many trees are going to be removed and how many replanted. Then she explains that she will pass the documents on to a landscape architect contracted by the management company to review the plan. The meeting ends quickly and the three leave, feeling the odd combination of relief and anxiety that follows a final exam.

About two weeks later, Joni gets word that the review is in. The reviewing landscape architect calls to congratulate her on the plan's design. How was she able to get a big company to move so decisively away from the typical lawn-dominated landscape, he asks. Days later, the management company sends the final critique to Phil at HP. The reviewer's written remarks are glowing: "This design is one of the best we've seen for the corporate landscape."

Apprehension, even if just a small amount, is part of the

infrastructure of landscape designs. Landscape architects worry that clients won't like a design. Clients worry that neighbors, review boards, and permitting agencies won't like a design. And reviewers and permitting agents sweat the details that keep the plans within local design and safety codes. So each time someone praises the plan, the relief is almost palpable. Phil passes the review around the HP office and makes sure Steve Shokrai has a copy. "It kind of shows we're headed in the right direction," Phil says with delight. It gives Joni and Michael and the HP landscape project team a boost of confidence, a soothing bit of validation.

The weeks counting down to October 31 are filled with good news and bad news.

HP's deadline for subcontractor bids is mid-September and Phil and Ted think they might be able to break ground before the end of that month. "I'm anxious to break ground because the weather is nice now," Phil says. California's rainy season officially begins in October, although the rainiest days usually don't hit until December or later. It would be ideal to complete most of the construction before the end of the year and get plants into the ground in time for their first watering by winter rains. But these hopes seem to vanish when the construction bids are higher than anyone expected and higher than the company has budgeted—even after revising its budget upward. Complicating matters further, HP managers feel the demolition will disturb the workers in Buildings 2, 4, and 6, so they decide the demoliton should be done on weekends. Weekend time is overtime for construction workers, and this adds more cost to the project. Joni and the HP team will have to make some fast decisions to get the landscape within budget without losing time.

About half the cost increase comes from optional lights under trees that the lighting consultant included in his estimates. Joni, Ted, and Phil reaffirm Joni's earlier decision not to include those lights in this phase. That alone won't cover all the added dollars, so the trio reluctantly decide to cut Deer Path. That leaves only Salmon Run among the three walking paths originally designed to give employees a safer journey across the parking lot.

Finally, by the end of September, the task of paring costs appears to be complete and HP's money managers sign off on the project. This simple move is better than the *Good Housekeeping* seal of approval for Joni. The project met the crucial funding deadline a month early and will get built.

There is no real celebration, though, and no groundbreaking yet, because the plans are still at the city, waiting for permits to clear. The project is small enough that it won't have to go through a formal design review presentation before the city's architectural review board. This means the city staff can take care of it in less time than usual. Before they can issue a building permit, though, the city staff wants details about how much new water the landscape will draw from the public water system. The landscape is going to be hooked up to HP's new water-reclamation system, which will take water used in manufacturing and research, clean out impurities, then pump it into tanks for irrigation. But if HP shuts its system down for service, the city wants to know how much city water will be used to supplement the reclaimed supply.

By early October, Ted submits the permit applications and information about the water-reclamation system to the city. Finally, during Halloween week, the permits come through.

Almost exactly one year since Joni first submitted a design proposal to Hewlett-Packard, groundbreaking is just days away. Construction equipment starts pulling into the HP parking lot and workers erect temporary fences to keep pedestrians out of the work area, and begin marking where asphalt will be cut. On the first Saturday in November, the first construction worker makes the first assault on the concrete, cutting it along the marked lines with a power saw. Three days later, Joni rushes into Palo Alto for an emergency meeting with Ted, Phil, and Charlie Ramone, the construction foreman for the landscape. Everything suddenly seems to be going wrong.

A lab group in Building 4 has surfaced, saying that it was never informed about the landscape project. The group brings heavy equipment into the building several times a year. It needs access for that equipment through Acorn Court. Another group of employees, fond of a large pepper tree, has learned that the tree is slated for removal and makes a complaint. On the site, workers discover that existing electrical boxes haven't been installed properly and will have to be dug up and reinstalled. And early soil tests worry the contractor; he asks HP to do more tests to make sure the soil under the asphalt isn't contaminated.

"We're trying to work through the details," a tired-sounding Ted says after the emergency meeting. Joni will have to redesign the entrance to Acorn Court, the one court that until now had required the fewest modifications from the original plan. The pepper tree will likely have to stay. The electrical boxes will have to be reinstalled. The soil could present the biggest problem or the biggest false alarm, but he won't know until the company's soil-remediation experts have a chance to look at it. In any case, he concludes, these last-minute problems are par for the course on a big project.

Joni is not happy about the latest developments. It means more delays and more changes to a plan that she has already changed more times than she likes. "As soon as you start to do things, people come out of the woodwork," she says, sighing.

Joni has heard that each time the project is slowed, her team is being blamed within the HP offices. She worries that Janecki & Associates is being the scapegoat, even when delays have nothing to do with her work. She isn't on the site every day and she knows it's easy to blame someone who is not there. Clients, contractors, and landscape architects share a mutual dependence that creates a kind of love-hate relationship. If problems aren't solved right away, it leans more toward hate. So when she hears rumors of finger-pointing, she has taken to calling the complainants immediately to clear the air. The next best thing to being there, she finds, is being a phone call away.

After the meeting on these latest snafus, Joni heads toward Santa Cruz and stops at a restaurant with a beach-side deck. She sits on the sunny deck, eats a salad for lunch, and sketches some ideas for the new Acorn Court. Later, she will pass the sketches to Michael, who will create formal drawings and incorporate the new design into the construction blueprints.

For a moment, she watches volleyball players practicing a few yards away. A life of beach volleyball looks very appealing right now. Then she gathers her sketches and leaves to go to her computer to write a memo to Ted about the changes discussed at the meeting this morning. They will affect the paving, the plan layout, the irrigation and lighting. They will also add to the cost. "I'm paranoid that this will reflect on us," she says later. "So I'm going to put it all in writing now."

Hundreds of miles to the south in Montecito, the Sands faced new sets of delays on their landscape. Winter rains were rougher on the Sands' house than the couple realized. Their new drain system worked like a charm where it had been installed. But in one spot near the front door and under the old front porch that had been inaccessible to installers, late season rains managed to settle, causing one part of the foundation to sink. The Sands poured more time and more money into fixing the foundation. They began the summer determined to build that front fence and driveway to get some privacy. But as the end of the season approaches, they change their minds.

"We've talked to some people and they've convinced us we should go from the house out," Dennis says one clear August day. So the couple turn their attention to building two porches, one at the front door and another off a sunroom on the side farthest from the street. "Then from there we can start moving out," Dennis explains. "After that, we might start doing the wall, the front gate, the driveway, etc. And then, from that, we can start doing our walkways, and then we can start planting."

Originally, the house had brick porches attached to the front and the side of the house. Now the porches are disheveled and their bricks, old red squares no longer routinely manufactured, are broken apart. Dennis and Abbe decide to make the new porch several inches higher to meet the front door better. They will replace the brick with some kind of stone, but they don't know exactly what. Off and on over several weeks, they travel around town looking at existing walkways and patios and they peruse magazines and books, searching for the perfect stone.

"We basically know the look we want," Dennis says. They want a stone that will blend with their home's tan hues, a stone that looks more like California and less like old New England. They want something like the buff-colored flagstone they've admired in different places around Santa Barbara, most notably at its courthouse. So they begin to talk to stone dealers, visiting a handful of businesses whose yards are decorated with bins of stone dug from distant quarries, waiting to be trucked to customers.

By early fall, though, the Sands begin to change their minds once again. They decide two small porches won't do the job. A friend whose taste they admire makes a powerful suggestion. Revise Joni's landscape plan just a bit and increase the front porch to a big wraparound, the friend says. Put the first landscape work into the porch. You'll always have plenty of space for entertaining, she tells Abbe. You'll never regret it.

There is something magnetic about a big porch with a grand view, a porch long enough to support a small roller skater, wide enough to become an impromptu dance floor. Originally, the Sands had encouraged Joni to design with costs in mind and instructed her to keep porches small. But now they could see themselves enjoying lounging on a big porch. Plus the porch had practical appeal. By building it along the entire front of the house, they could ensure water would not settle against what had proven to be a trouble spot for their home's foundation.

"Then I called Joni and said, 'Joni, what do you think about this?' And she said, 'There's nothing better than a wraparound porch,' " Abbe recalls one October morning as she watches craftsman Larry Hochhalter work on the porch foundation. "It sort of evolved like everything else we've ever done."

First Abbe and Dennis considered having Joni draft a design and construction details for the porch. But, to keep costs down, they decided instead to figure the wraparound's dimensions and design themselves. Hochhalter assured them he could work from their rough idea to create a rock-solid porch.

Hochhalter had already helped the Sands restore and remodel two homes, including this one. Intelligent and even-tempered, he has spent most of his adult life doing custom building and remodeling, framing a home here, reworking a driveway there. His penchant for precision and attention to detail has attracted a stable of demanding upscale clients. He had never laid a flagstone porch before, but with a quick tutorial from a mason, he figured he could do this job just as well as he had done any other in his career.

And so the Sands put in orders for flagstone from a California quarry and complementary steps and stone caps from a Kansas quarry. Hochhalter went to work on the porch foundation, framing it with concrete block, reinforcing it with rebar, and then topping it with a truckload of poured concrete. Atop this finished foundation, he would fit the flagstone like puzzle pieces, holding them in place with concrete mortar.

"We'll have a four-inch cap all the way around, so there'll be a border," Abbe says just days before the concrete is poured and weeks before the final loads of stone arrive. When all is done, the block foundation will be barely visible, obscured by a dirt berm that will slope into the front yard.

While they were planning the porch, the Sands expanded their first construction phase to include landscaping part of the yard. Once the porch is finished, they will have an irrigation specialist lay a sprinkler system through most of the yard and then plant a traditional turf-grass lawn. "We want a big lawn in front of the house and it will sort of be outlined by the trees," Dennis explains as he joins Abbe beside the porch-in-progress. Fresh from a morning bicycle ride, he is relaxed and buoyant as he describes the new plans. Between the oval outline of trees and the lawn, the Sands plan a meadow of grasses and wildflowers, a nod to the landscape Joni had planned. "So we'll have a regular lawn here and then behind it higher grass and it'll look real pretty . . . It's the quickest, easiest, and at this point the cheapest way to get out of this dirt mode that we're in now." It will also give Dennis something he only lately realized was part of his vision of paradise: a lawn on which to play catch with his son, where dirt and gravel won't bite and chew a baseball or steal it for good

The Sands' decision to put in a lawn, the American landscape's most enduring symbol of neighborhood conformity, almost seems to surprise the couple as they admit it to a visitor. "We didn't think we would ever want lawn, because we came from a very dry climate and we thought it's just not meant to be on the desert floor. Well, here it's conducive to just growing anything, and so we can bring in lawn. And now that's all we want," Abbe says. "And I even want flowers now! I was one of those who said, 'Roses? Yech.' And now I've gotten old and I want them. I want color. I've lived in the dirt too long. Before, we lived with these rosebushes and I said, 'Get them out of here.' So, you never know," she concludes with a shrug. "It's sort of a mood thing more than anything."

The old plans to have a native-dominated garden have mostly floated away with the end of a years-long drought. As they have for so many, natives have become synonymous in the Sands' minds with waterwise gardening and not much else. "When we first moved here, there was a drought and it was a real consideration," Abbe says, taking a seat on a sample stack of cut stone that resemble huge edible chunks of halvah. Lately, though, the newspapers have carried stories about local water authorities having more water than expected after a wetter-than-normal year. Now the natives seem less appealing to the couple. Like so many homeowners across the country, the Sands now think they will go with the mostly exotic plants that have become keystones of the proper American homesite.

Remnants of Joni's plan are still discernible in the Sands' future landscape. They still expect to incorporate the driveway, an arbor, and the front fence the landscape architect planned. They also want to put in the niche she designed for a hidden corner of the finished garden, a small spot set aside to discover and relax. Someday they will have Joni detail a planting plan, perhaps taking into account Abbe's newfound appreciation of roses. But for now, at least, the Sands' landscape budget will go into the wraparound porch and the lawn. The rest will wait.

XIV

IF YOU'RE A PEDIATRICIAN AND HALF OF YOUR PAtients die before they reach adulthood, something is terribly wrong. If you're an auto mechanic and half the cars that leave your garage break down on the drive home, it is safe to say you are a failure in your trade. If you're a landscape architect and half the projects you design never get built, you're in good company.

Consider the case of the Olmsteds. After Frederick Sr. retired in 1895, Frederick Jr. took over the family firm and ran it until 1957. For one hundred years, an Olmsted put his distinctive imprint on America's landscape. As Olmsted authority Charles Beveridge notes, in all that time the Olmsteds were commissioned for about six thousand projects, only about half of which were actually built. Yet most landscape architects regard the Olmsteds as both prolific and successful.

One of the truths of landscape architecture is that a lot of designs never go beyond the paper on which they are drafted.

So the ones that do get executed become that much more precious to their designer. They are the gold medals that make all the unmedaled races seem worth it. They are the successes that ease the nagging fear that the next project will fail. Sometimes clients understand this. On a day when nothing seemed to go quite right, Joni was chatting with Ted Dukelow at Hewlett-Packard when one of Ted's colleagues familiar with the landscape project approached them both. You have to make sure this thing gets done, he told Ted. This project isn't any good to you, Joni, if you don't have something to photograph. It has to get done.

Indeed, if landscape architects had their way, all the projects would get done. And they would be maintained. They would last forever, like the statue of David or the Mona Lisa. They would be the world's outdoor artwork, protected and cherished, and, above all, finished.

On a cloudy December day sixteen months after Joni first visited the Sands' home, Abbe and Dennis aren't so sure about that wraparound porch and front lawn, after all. In fact, they're ready to drop the idea entirely. "I'm telling you, as of yesterday, we were going to break it all down and do Joni's plan," an exasperated Abbe says. They've run into problems with the stone, and the whole project is becoming twice as expensive as they planned. The cost of the porch alone keeps rising, now to at least $50,000 and possibly more, because the price of the stone could be as much as three times greater than what their stone dealer led them to believe. "We try to be as methodical and thorough as possible," Abbe says with a sigh, "but these stone guys are not."

The Sands' plans for the porch seemed to be unfolding smoothly until a truck delivered the first bins of flat, buff-colored stone. As Larry Hochhalter inspected the bins, he realized they contained pavers, a much smaller version of the flagstone the couple believed they had ordered. Dennis got on the phone to the stone broker, who admitted he had made a mistake. He would get them flagstone, but he had only two bins in stock, a small fraction of what they needed for the porch. It would take a few weeks to get the rest. By the way, the broker added, he had also misquoted the price. The flagstone would be much more expensive. Effortlessly, it seemed, the broker had managed to drop two bombshells at once.

Dennis considered his options. He could tell the broker to forget the whole deal, but then the half-finished porch would sit that way for who knows how long, while the Sands tracked down another stone dealer. Or Dennis could postpone a decision while he absorbed the impact of the bad news. Dennis picked option two with a twist. He told the broker to send a truck to pick up the pavers and bring out one bin of flagstone. He wanted to see for himself what the more expensive flagstones looked like. He also wanted to have a bin of the good stones to compare with other bins if the couple decided to order more.

Now the wire-sided bin of flagstones, about two tons' worth, sits like a hostage in the yard as the Sands try to decide what to do next. They must decide within two days whether to order an additional twenty tons of the stone. "Do we rethink the materials?" Abbe almost groans. To compound their aggravation, Abbe and Dennis have had to press the stone broker to give them a final price for the flagstone. "I don't think they really give you the price until you're locked into the numbers," she complains.

The Sands have also learned that they will need to buy more than they originally planned of a second variety of stone for the porch steps. As he prepared to lay the steps, Larry discovered that the quality of one sample pallet of the step stone shipped from Kansas—which the stone broker sold to them at a discount after another customer rejected it—was uneven. Some pieces are cut with the stone's natural grain, some against it.

"Maybe it's the nature of the business," Abbe says philosophically. The Sands will probably decide to continue building the porch "after we've got it all out of our systems—the anger," she says, because the porch still provides the best way to keep the water away from the foundation. But the higher price tag is also going to keep them from doing much else for several months. They will have to postpone installing a sprinkler system, putting in a lawn and a surrounding meadow, elements that would get rid of the mud. Abbe's hopes of seeing green by spring are dashed. "I'm so disappointed," she says as she looks out over the yard on a chilly gray day. "If you just look out at the top of the trees, you can almost see how it might look."

A few weeks later, just days after New Year's Eve, a workman aboard a forklift removes from a truck bed the last of several pallets of large stone blocks shipped from Kansas. He delivers it to the edge of the Sands' unfinished porch, where

Larry has already begun to lay out flagstone pieces. Only yards away, five pallets of flagstone delivered earlier sit waiting. Larry guides a diamond-bladed power saw along one piece of flagstone, smoothing its edge as he cuts. A paper mask protects his nose and mouth from inhaling the fine stone dust the saw shoots into the air. He stops his saw, removes his mask, and saunters over to inspect the Kansas stone that will become the porch's steps and edges. Abbe finishes a phone call in the house and then comes out to see the delivered goods.

After a few minutes' inspection, Larry pronounces the new stone perfect. Then, unable to resist a taste of the future, one by one he lifts two heavy but manageable pieces of the rectangular stone and positions them next to each other along the edge of the porch. The blocks have been cut at the quarry to fit the edge exactly and their faces have been chipped with chisels to give them a stylish finish. He stands back to see the effect. "Oh, it's beautiful," Abbe says. It is just a beginning, but finally it seems that the porch will be completed.

For much of the next three months, Larry methodically cuts and shapes the flagstone into pieces that fit neatly together on the porch surface. He does much of the work alone. But sometimes he hires a day laborer to help. He has never worked with stone like this before, but he quickly gets into a rhythm: fit, cut, fit again, remove, cement, fit one last time. Once all the flagstone pieces have been laid out, he places the Kansas stone along the edges and on the few wide steps leading from the yard to the porch, and then from the porch to the front door. One day, to satisfy his curiosity, Larry pours a cup of water out on the porch where it meets the house. The water rolls easily away from the house. The porch drains beautifully and the builder is satisfied.

"It's an accomplishment," Larry says about doing construction, just hours before finishing the last task on the porch. "It's not like working in the post office, where tomorrow you have to do it again." At the end of his workday, he has a product that he can see and touch.

On one unusually warm day in late March, he has a magnificent wraparound porch to his credit. He finishes it by mopping the flagstone with an acid wash to remove lime residue left behind by the cement grout. Behind him, as he mops, leftover flagstone pieces sit in a pile in the yard. Beyond the pile, weeds that have sprouted over the winter sway gently with the slightest breeze.

On a perfect evening two weeks later, the Sands celebrate Dennis's birthday with a small family dinner on the porch. Abbe has mixed emotions about the porch. "Oh, we love it," she says a few days later. But she adds that sticker shock still lingers. And this project, because it was so long and slow and filled with obstacles, ranks as the most difficult the Sands have tackled in their years of homestead improvement. Enjoying the porch feels almost mandatory and has become a family joke. "Get out on the patio!" is now Dennis's favorite command. "In the long run, we'll be happy," Abbe says, adding with a laugh, "We take full responsibility for our actions."

There is still so much to do. The yard is without a finished landscape; the hodgepodge of see-through fencing that borders the street continues to allow a full view into their lives. Already the couple is thinking about what to do next. And before another season passes, workers begin a new phase on the Montecito landscape. The Sands' drive to finish their yard is strong and they call in an irrigation expert to lay a grid of irrigation pipes throughout the yard, a bulldozer to grade it, a lawn company to seed grass and wildflowers, and Larry to begin work on the front fence and driveway.

"You know, it was sort of just looking like the Beverly Hillbillies. Even Den said it sort of became an embarrassment," Abbe says one morning as she waits for an inspector to arrive to check some new electrical lines just installed. The yard is a maze of deep trenches, some carrying electrical lines, some carrying irrigation pipes. A few days earlier, the irrigation installer tested the new system. "We almost cried when they tried the water out, when it went on. It was so exciting," she continues. "You know, we've been watching the progress of people that come into this neighborhood and have the financial wherewithal to be able to come in and just do it. And I'm thinking, 'It's not as satisfying.' " She lifts her chin high into a lighthearted imitation of self-satisfaction and then laughs.

On this phase, Abbe and Dennis plan to use Joni's design for the driveway with its elliptical parking pad outlined by orange trees. They also expect to bring her in to create a planting plan for the section between the new fence and the street. Eucalyptus trees alone stand there and Abbe worries that "it's going to be a tough call to find the right plant that's going to grow. I'd like that to be really something that is not scruffy-looking." She compares her concern about the plantings on the street side of the fence to the film world. "Let the props be on the outside and we can deal with what's in the inside."

Until now, the Sands have incorporated into their landscape little of Joni's master plan for their mesa-top property. But that plan came to the Sands shortly after they moved into their home, before they had spent a full year there and had time to learn its quirks, learn where water drained, where it didn't, what bothered them, what didn't. Since then, they have learned that their foundation needed more protection from the rains than they realized. They have learned that their house's sewer system needed major repairs, requiring heavy trenching across their land. Their taste for lawn has increased. Given all the things they learned later, does Abbe regret that they bothered to have a landscape plan done so soon after they moved into the house? Not really, she says.

The plan gave them a road map from which they felt free to make detours to accommodate their new knowledge about themselves and their property. It also gave them hope on those days when it looked as if they would never have a finished landscape. "I don't think it was jumping the gun to have it," Abbe concludes. "I think it got us thinking: Is this going to work out? What about that pole? etc." It gave them a goal.

Joni gets her first view of the wraparound porch in a snapshot as she works in her Santa Cruz office. "It's beautiful," she says, examining the photo. She has always wanted a wraparound porch herself, so she understands the Sands' decision. She is disappointed to learn that lawn will replace the native and drought-tolerant plants she recommended, foliage that could give birds and insects the habitat the lawn can't provide. But she is resigned to having little control over the end result in owner-installed landscapes. In any landscape project, money, patience, and a client's own tastes can easily overrule a landscape architect's vision for paradise. This becomes even more true when the client is doubling as installer or contractor, figuratively and sometimes literally driving the bulldozer and wielding the shovel. They have to do what makes them happy, Joni says. She'll stand ready to offer advice when they want it.

Eighteen months after the first crew of Salinas schoolchildren planted the first fledgling oak in the new Natividad Creek Park, the park is still unfinished. Workers must paint lines on the tennis courts; two walking bridges spanning the creek are under construction; the playground with swing sets is still encircled by a temporary fence to discourage its use. Yet, in fits and starts, sixty-four acres of open space along the creek have metamorphosed from damaged creek banks, scarred slopes, and denuded fields into a tangible, usable gathering and playing place for people from the neighborhood and beyond.

The temporary fence around the playground is more show than anything else. Shortly after it goes up, some silent communal urge to climb on the swings causes part of the fence to topple over and workers decide not to bother repairing it, figuring it will only be pushed over again. Neighbors who had worried the park might become a gang haven even before it could be completed have banded together to protect their park. Each evening at nine, a small group of adults strolls through to make sure all is quiet.

Late one afternoon, hours after schools have let out for

the day and builders have wheeled their trucks out of the park, several children sit on the swings. They engage in that soul-freeing repetitive leg push that drives the swings higher and higher until it seems almost possible to touch the blue in the sky. Just beyond the playground, two adolescent boys push a bicycle down a slope and disappear behind the trees and shrubs that line the once-barren creek bed. Shortly, they emerge on the other side with the bike. A worn trail suggests this is not a new routine, the day the bridges are completed can't come too soon.

Ed Piper rolls into the parking lot in his truck, prepared to take a visitor on a four-wheel tour through the park. He is grinning broadly, proud of what this place is becoming. He drives the truck up over a curb and along a pathway that doubles as a service road. He complains when a turning radius isn't large enough to accommodate his vehicle without taking out a sprinkler head and notes that it will have to be changed. When he comes to a spot where he can get a good view of the slope that the schoolchildren planted so many months ago, he stops for a moment and squints toward it. The trees look good. Most have survived and grown, and some of the native bunch grasses are clearly flourishing. On the other side of the pathway, he can see the creek bank that is now thick with shrubs and grasses planted by community members and more schoolchildren. Too many weeds, mostly exotic grasses, have sprouted, but a Weedwacker can take care of that, he figures.

This half of the park is designated for intensive use. The natural landscape Joni's firm created for it is thickest along the creek and on the hillside. It is background and filler.

Scattered throughout the flatland between the hillside and the creek, and between the creek and the street, are picnic tables and benches, an amphitheater, a volleyball pit, tennis courts. Soon there will be a BMX bicycle course for kids, but until it is built, Ed figures it will be hard to chase the bike acrobats out of the creek.

Although this park is incomplete, most of the planting is done. Nature here is on a path to a strong recovery. Nowhere is this more obvious than on the side of the park separated from the parking lots and the play courts by a road and linked to it by a tunnel. On that side, natural landscape is a star.

Ed steers his truck through the short tunnel and suddenly the windshield view is filled with a wilder world. Less than two years ago, floods scoured the creek bank nearly bare. Years of human intervention had channeled most of the creek into nothing more than a ditch. Now, after grading to widen the creek's spread and after multiple planting parties by Return of the Natives, the bank is thick with growth. Here and there ponds have formed and sedges and rushes signal their existence. Willows and oaks, some new, some remnants from the past, form a not too distant backdrop. For a moment, if you keep your eyes within the park's borders—if you don't look too far to the right or left, where new housing developments erupt from scraped and terraced earth—it looks and feels as if time has crept back and nature has leapt ahead. This once-moribund place is now alive. Red-winged blackbirds dive in and out of the plants. Scarlet mayflies dart about like living helicopters. There are sounds that don't belong to any machine. Birdcalls, insect buzzes, wing flaps. The air is fragrant: Is it sage or a combination of dozens of different wild plants?

During his tour, Ed is asked if this is the way he expected this park to look. He wastes no time answering. "I knew it was going to look natural," he says. "I hope it's what everyone else expected."

This is not a *House & Garden* environment. It does not call to mind most garden-center displays. This is not the sort of place promoted by the mainstream of America's gardening culture with its devotion to newness, exotica, bold statements, massive color, and generally anything that contrasts with the more subtle landscapes found in the country's diminishing wildlands. This is a restoration, a landscape returned to its past. And for a moment it seems to restore the visitor as well.

Historians and nature writers have produced reams of pages defining and speculating about the changing relationship of people to nature. Nowhere, it seems, has anyone tried or been able to establish how what we see every day in the created landscape—from suburban front lawns to potted plantings in urban office courtyards—affects our attitude toward nature. But it seems clear that, as a group, we humans are at best oblivious to what we have never seen and don't know, and at worst frightened by it. If we don't see created landscapes that reflect local and regional wildlands, their plants and design, then what do we lose in knowledge about and sympathy for the diminishing wildlands, especially if the beauty in those wildlands is subtle?

Many gardeners, no matter how avid, cannot go into a wild area and name more than a plant or two. In places like Southern California and Florida, where the built landscape is mostly patterned after something that never existed in the wild in those regions, relatively few people can identify specific wildland plants. When asked about native plants, one California-based buyer for a national chain of garden centers dismissed the idea. Just look at the scrubby hills, he said, there's nothing worth having in the garden. Yet people who know the plants native to that region argue otherwise.

Aside from taste in flora, the most profound thing separating people who want to include natives in their landscapes from those who don't is that one knows the plants—from their names to their place in the ecosystem—and the other does not. If you don't know the plants, if when you look at a wild hillside all you can see is a scrubby mess instead of a distinctive, rich, beautiful plant community, why would you ever think to include those wild things in your garden, much less in your garden center?

Knowing the names, the look, and the habits of the native plants makes a wild place more familiar, less frightening, more precious. In a way, people like Joni Janecki, Ed Piper, and the people at Hewlett-Packard who dared to deviate from the typical corporate landscape are doing more than giving the world attractive landscapes. They are helping people learn about wildland plants, teaching us the natural history of a place. As far as Ed Piper is concerned, the thick new growth along the Natividad Creek bank, the birds and insects that have returned, the feeling of space and identifiable place, are simple benefits of such teaching.

As much as Joni, Michael, Ted, and Phil wanted to see the Hewlett-Packard landscape realized, for months the fates seemed to be working against them. True, there was some tangible achievement. New soil tests came back clean and cleared the way for demoliton to continue and construction to begin. Workers using saws and bulldozers removed the unwanted asphalt and sent eleven truckloads to be recycled. They started pushing dirt around with tractors, grading and forming sinuous berms in Acorn Court even before all the blacktop was gone from the site, partly to make sure HP brass and employees could see some progress. But then nature took over. The winter rains arrived.

"Water, water everywhere," Ted said with resignation in mid-December after several days of steady showers. Where bulldozers scraped away asphalt, the heavy rains formed puddles and ponds. After a few days, the soil began to dry, but then more rain came. Workers couldn't continue grading and trenching for electrical lines and irrigation or building forms and pouring concrete until the soil dried. The project was already behind schedule by about a week, according to Ted's estimation, and the rains would set it back by at least another week. Best case, if the rain stopped soon, the project might be finished by the first week in March. Plants would be blooming in the new landscape by spring. But, Ted joked as the rain fell, "it may be wild rice."

Unfortunately, the rains returned periodically, and between showers water remained trapped on the excavated areas, creating what one wag called Lake Packard. Even on sunny days, buildings 2, 4, and 6 cast winter shadows over the site, further slowing the drying of the soil.

During dry spells, workers were able to complete some tasks, such as forming concrete footings for concrete-cast benches, and Michael would drive to the site on Fridays to meet with Phil and the contractor's foreman to go over any details that needed to be smoothed out. Most weeks, though, little got done, because of the rain. By the end of March, the project was still far from finished. But there was good news: the shadows were receding, the rain had stopped, and the site was finally beginning to dry.

As the HP project shifts into the construction phase at long last, Joni hands over most of the client contact and weekly meetings with the contractor at HP to Michael. It is a lot of responsibility for a fellow who was finishing up his landscape-architecture degree just over a year earlier. Joni doesn't think it is the ideal arrangement. She would rather attend the meetings herself than delegate. But she has to use her staff's time and her own efficiently.

Projects seem to be flowing into the firm now. Almost overnight, the mellow little practice isn't so mellow or so little anymore. It has about a dozen projects under construction and five more at various stages of design. They cover just about every kind of commission, from small-scale urban planning to residential-garden design to ecological restoration. And lately, a couple of plum projects, including one in tandem with a top American architect, have come to the firm unsolicited, giving Joni an ego boost shot through with apprehension.

Each new project is "exciting at the beginning," she says. But each involves design and planning, "and it becomes work and you have to get it finished and have to do a good job—well, it also comes with anxiety." As the firm's workload increases, Joni has less time to spend on each project herself, and the pressure on the rest of the staff to get as much done in a day as possible grows.

Robin especially is feeling restive as she watches the firm change. The entire profession "has kind of got this desperation to it," she observes. More than just about anyone else on any construction project—more than the mason, more than the engineer—the landscape architects are "constantly having to justify the need for their fees," she says. The pressure is on landscape architects to work fast and keep the number of hours devoted to designing or drawing up construction documents, or any of the steps in between, as low as possible.

Joni thinks about adding another staff member. On the one hand, the firm needs the help. On the other hand, she worries whether she can keep the work flowing in to cover the paychecks. "I haven't quite figured out how you get bigger," she muses. Most of what Joni has learned about the business end of landscape architecture has come on the job, but she still doesn't have the answers she thinks she needs to do it as well as she wants to. "I don't even know how much I'm supposed to be making a year," she says.

Except for the almost weekly drive into Palo Alto, Michael

doesn't seem to mind taking on full duty for the HP project. With the end of the winter rains and the arrival of spring, construction moves quickly. Courtyard by courtyard, workers install irrigation pipes and electrical lines and pour fresh concrete. They remove protective fences as concrete dries, and before the entire landscape is complete, HP employees are able to use its pathways to come and go to the three buildings.

On the second day of summer, Michael makes his weekly visit to the site. He carries blueprints and looks at the ground as he walks through the landscape-in-progress, eyeing the new concrete. The pathways and seating areas that form Acorn Court and the curving sidewalk that forms Salmon Run are now finished. The planting is still not done, though, and there are piles of dirt between the courtyards and the pathways. Some have been smoothed and gently mounded; some are untouched.

"I was here Monday and showed them how to berm some of Acorn and left instructions for the rest," Michael says as he examines the areas waiting to be planted. Left on their own, the workmen tend to interpret the blueprints so literally that they make the dirt piles almost square, not creating the rounded, serpentine look the landscape architects envision. "Joni is really concerned about getting the berms right."

The concrete for Deer Court's hardscape remains unpoured. A wiry, deeply tanned workman wearing a billed cap puts finishing touches on the thin wooden forms that outline where concrete will be poured. The forms will hold the concrete in place until it dries. A grid of steel reinforcement wire rests on the bottom of the forms against the dirt that the concrete will cover. If the workman has made any mistakes interpreting the plans, this is the time to correct them, when correction means readjusting a board here or there rather than chipping out and repouring concrete.

Michael stares for a moment at one section where a board creates the outline of a curved edge. He wonders if the outline is supposed to be a straight edge. "This isn't quite what we were going for," he says softly, then moves to the sidewalk and unrolls the plans on the flat surface, kneels and studies them. A moment later he cheerfully rolls up the plans and stands upright. "It's okay," he says.

Charlie Ramone, a round-faced, big-bellied man who seems almost a Central Casting choice for construction foreman, strides with purpose down the pathway toward Michael, who smiles and asks how things are going. So far, so good today, Charlie says, and then moves on to confer with a team of workmen installing electrical lines for lighting.

Michael's job at this point makes him by necessity a nuisance. He is responsible for pointing out defects to make sure the job is done right. This quiet, novice landscape architect, young enough to be Charlie's kid, is now responsible for telling the veteran builder where his workers have erred, what they need to fix. Early in the job, Michael seemed almost intimidated by Charlie and his boss, Bob Benson. Now, after months of working with the builders, Michael appears almost at ease with the reticent foreman.

Michael has learned a lot about construction on this job, the first he has ever followed from design through execution. In this project, for instance, he designed a lot of curves and flares into the new concrete pathways, particularly where they meet other pathways. While watching the design being implemented, he has learned that the flares are harder for workmen to do successfully with their stiff wooden forms and concrete than are simple squared ends. In the future, he says, "I'm sure I'll design differently."

After inspecting the site, Michael approaches Charlie and seems almost reluctant to have to report a couple of spots the workers will need "to fine-tune." The older man follows Michael to the far end of Cougar Den, where the designer points out a two-foot-wide strip workers missed when they poured concrete. The foreman squints at the spot and then inspects the blueprint. "That's a little thing," he finally concludes. It can be easily repaired. The air and mood lighten.

"Well, by the middle of next week, we won't have to worry about concrete," Charlie cheerily notes as the two men stroll back to the center of the site. "It'll just be shaping and planting." By the end of June or the beginning of July, he estimates, the whole project will be done.

Weeks before that final day, though, Joni's firm gets some bad news. Phil Koenig will be leaving the project June 1 to take a new job with HP at its Cupertino office. His position at the Palo Alto site will be phased out within a matter of months as part of a general belt-tightening company-wide and his duties overseeing the headquarters' landscape will go to an outside contractor.

Phil is delighted and relieved to find another job within HP. Michael and Joni are not thrilled to learn he will be leaving before the project is done. He has been a key booster and a reliable contact skilled at overseeing construction projects, often unofficially taking the lead on project management and following up on critical details. As it happens, by the time the new landscape is finished, few of its early promoters at the company are still involved.

Just days before the landscape's completion, Ted Dukelow walks with Charlie along a pathway through Deer Court. The low-key water feature in Acorn Court is finished, and the imitation boulders the fountain maker created have been scattered in the planting areas among grasses, trees, and shrubs. Most of the plants have been planted, though some are still to be delivered. Ted stops for a moment and notices three redwood trees in one area. The immature trees are only about six feet tall, with stick-like trunks. Beneath them, a couple of dozen ferns seem to be wilting under the unremorseful heat of the midday sun. About half the year, during fall and winter, the building shades this spot, but there is nothing to protect the ferns at this time of year. Ted likes the landscape so far, he says, but he is worried about the ferns. It's too bad the trees aren't bigger, he says.

As one landscape architect is fond of telling clients about plants in a new landscape, the first year they sleep, the second year they creep, and the third year they leap. The problem this time is that the redwoods planted to provide summer shade won't be big enough in time to save the ferns. Had the construction not been delayed, planting would have been done in the winter, which would have given the ferns a season to grow strong enough to better tolerate the sun. Only time will tell if they will survive the next few months.

Workers completed the HP landscape in early July. Just as construction had begun with no fanfare, so did it end. There were no ribbons cut, no champagne bottles broken, no flags hoisted, no outward celebration. There was just another workday when HP employees arrived early as usual, emptied from their parked cars, scurried along the landscape's pathways and into the buildings that house their desks and computers.

Nearly two years passed between the day HP began soliciting bids from landscape architects for the project and the day the last construction worker left. The project took longer than Steve Shokrai expected and much longer than he liked. Once it was finished, though, he remained convinced the company had picked the right design and the right designer. With the plants still immature, it would be a year or two before the landscape's full effect would be felt, but "from my point of view it looks pretty nice," Steve said two months after the last workman left. "It's different. People have to get used to it because it's not really a stereotype corporate landscape. It's more like a natural landscape than like some kind of artificial, stereotype lawn. It looks more like natural views that you see in California."

Some of the plants—including the ferns—are wilting and look as if they might be dead, he says, but there is still time to replace them. Most of the comments he has heard from employees are favorable, and that pleases him. Still, one thing troubles Steve. People aren't using the seating areas as he had hoped they would; they aren't pausing to enjoy the new courtyards. If they are enjoying this new paradise, it is mostly from afar.

One late September Saturday, Joni arrives at HP with a camera in hand, prepared to show a visitor through the new landscape while she snaps her first roll of photos of the finished project. She is wearing a white blouse that buttons off-center and black walking shorts. Her husband, Drew, who has driven over from Santa Cruz with her, leaves her a bottle of water and a wide-brimmed straw hat before he takes off to run some errands at a nearby shopping center.

She seems more relaxed than usual and is eager to show off the landscape, her firm's largest completed project to date, its urban resurrection of nature. Before she steps into the heart of the landscape, though, she pauses at the edge near where Salmon Run meets Acorn Court. A patch of turf block—a skeleton of blocks that have been recessed into the ground and planted with tufts of native grasses—lies beside the small water-reclamation facility that is hidden within a rectangle of fences. The patch will occasionally serve as a driveway for trucks pulling up to service the reclamation plant's tanks and machinery.

But something is not right. The turf block and its grasses are covered with a layer of bright white sand. At first Joni frowns. Then, shaking her head, she chuckles. The contractor was supposed to lay the sand under the block, not atop it. For a moment, she ponders why it was done this way, but then decides she will never understand. The sandy layer just illustrates why landscape architects "have to specify everything" in detailed notes on their construction drawings and planting plans. Now the contractor will have to remove the sandy layer and replace it with a mulch of ground wood chips as used on the rest of the landscape.

Joni snaps a shot of the turf block for the record and then strolls a few yards to Acorn Court's woodlands and then on through Deer Court's grassland meadow and Cougar Den's combination savanna and chaparral. She knows Steve's concern about the health of some of the plants and is prepared to find a disaster. But she finds that the problem plants are few and not as dramatic as rumored. "There are some dead plants," she says as she walks a pathway leading around a berm planted with ferns and young redwoods. "I was really expecting to see it looking like deadsville out here. But it's not like that."

Indeed, the landscape looks young but healthy and alive. Rolling berms, serpentine pathways, meadows, and tiny forests provide a striking contrast to the hard-edged buildings, softening the view inside and out. Here and there, seating areas, most of them consisting of curved cast-cement benches, dot the courtyards.

A few of the ferns will have to be replaced, Joni notes, but many are in good shape. "They're not little angel ferns, they're monster ferns" that can withstand a good deal of sunlight, she says. "I think the ferns are going to be okay." Some of the meadow grasses are a buff color rather than green, partly because, she says, their roots dried too much during the planting. But she expects them to return to green within a few weeks. "I was showing the [maintenance] guys that they can go through and clean out the dead blades by combing them," she says, crouching and running her fingers through one tawny tuft. "Then you'll see a lot more green.

Some of them are already starting to pump out the green."

She is concerned, though, about a pair of Catalina ironwoods, trees with long-fingered leaves. The two on one edge of Acorn Court look brown, rather than green. Michael had advised the clients to reject the ironwoods when they arrived from the nursery because they looked unhealthy. Instead, they decided to try to nurse the trees along.

More than with most artwork, more than with a painting or a sculpture or even a building, the survival and health of a landscape architect's work depends upon somebody other than the artist. The landscape changes as plants grow, and it changes as caretakers revise it to accommodate new tastes or new needs. It also grows or dies depending upon the kind of maintenance it gets. Joni has watched fine landscapes, including her own designs, ruined because of poor maintenance. Residential clients and commercial clients—the shopping-center builders especially—are the most likely to ruin a landscape. "All of a sudden you'll see it all cut into a ball, or overwatered," she says. Overwatering is a common problem, especially for native landscapes that include plants which go through periods of summer dormancy. When the plants want water the least, people feel compelled to water the most. The best tactic for a landscape architect to protect a design once it has been installed is to keep in touch with its caretakers and lobby for its care.

As she walks through the landscape's three courtyards, snapping photos, Joni plays dual roles: one as designer, one as critic. This is typical of her reaction to one of her finished projects. She always sees something in her work that could have been done better. There might be a seating area that could have been more intimate, a plant selection that could have been more appropriate. She is always asking herself: is it interesting, is it meaningful, is it going to last? Of any design she has finished, she says, "I can look at it and then tear it apart."

Today she is mostly happy, even delighted, with what she sees. She climbs the stairs to a second-floor balcony that stretches across the fronts of Buildings 4 and 6, to get an overview of the landscape. From there, she can see two courtyards at once. Together they create a fluid tapestry that bears hints of Burle Marx. A curving meadow flows into a snaking sidewalk. A mounded woodland blends into a seating area. It's a fine design, but the plants are so young that a viewer can only imagine how it will look in two or three years when the meadows have filled in, the woodlands and savannas have filled out.

Joni has heard of Steve's concern that people aren't using the landscape. They are walking through it, but rarely coming out to sit in it. This time of year, much of the seating is still in direct sunlight most of the day. "It's not shady enough," Joni concludes back at ground level as she scans Acorn Court. There has been talk of putting out standing umbrellas, but none has appeared so far. Once the plants grow bigger, there will be more shade in the summer.

Shade, though, isn't the only thing that influences whether people actually use the landscape. "They don't really know what they're looking at," Joni speculates. "Everybody is kind of in awe and they don't know how to interact with this new space or what these spaces are intended for." She leans over and rubs her fingers on the soft leaves of a sage and then smells the minty residue. The engineers and accountants who work here need to know that they can touch the plants, she says, and that this is "a nature spot for them, for them to come out and watch the hummingbirds." She has pondered how to get that message to the HP employees; she thinks it may be critical to the landscape's long-term survival. "I think they need to understand it in order for it to be loved and appreciated and enjoyed." So far, nothing has come of her suggestion to provide landscape walking tours to employees. Lately, she and Ted have talked about adding a few discreetly placed interpretive plaques that would explain the different habitats and plant communities.

At the far edge of the woodland community in Acorn Court, where nothing but asphalt covered the ground just months ago, a lazy trickle now flows across the strong likeness of a Sierra foothill rock pockmarked with grinding holes. A feather left earlier by a mourning dove rests on a dry spot on the rock. Last week, Ted and several other HP employees saw a red-tailed hawk, majestic and steely-eyed, alight on the wet rock, apparently to rest and drink.

Joni lifts her camera to take photos of the tiny stream but freezes for a moment when a hummingbird, its wings beating too fast to see, buzzes out of nowhere to within a yard of the water. Suddenly, as though it realized it was being watched, the tiny bird buzzes away and alights on a young oak tree's branch. Then, again suddenly—hummingbirds seem to move no other way—the bird dips off the tree and hovers as it feeds from the yellow-orange bloom of a monkey flower plant.

Joni Janecki's firm has just entered its fifth year. It has

some big clients and some return clients. Her firm's reputation for creating landscapes that are attractive and sensitive to the environment is growing. Measured purely by the work Joni has completed and the work she has in hand, she is a successful landscape architect. But there is another measure of success that to Joni seems equally important—if not more important.

Sometimes, like today, she returns to a native-plant landscape she has designed that has finally made it from paper to earth. She sees the new life that has come to the place—butterflies, bees, birds. She sees that the plants she selected provide food and a place to nest. She sees a landscape that helps link the people to their region's natural and human history, that gives them a version of paradise. She looks at all the native plants she has helped bring to the created landscape. At that moment, as she takes in all that her landscape has contributed and attracted, she feels good about her work. Then, more than ever, she feels successful, as though her finished canvas has been hung in the world's most important art museum, to be enjoyed by its most discerning patrons. "When you hear there's been a hawk in the water feature and six people saw it—that's pretty good," she says. "It doesn't get much better."

Acknowledgments

Like landscape architecture, book writing is often a cooperative venture. Many people, more than I can acknowledge by name within a page or two, helped me as I learned about the world of plants and landscape. All should know that I appreciate the time and information they gave, even though my impressions and conclusions may sometimes differ from their own.

Several provided help that was critical to this project. The most obvious of these are Joni Janecki and her colleagues Robin MacLean, Michael Bliss, Judy Titchenal, Jack Kiesel, and Amy West. Their cheerful patience as they answered yet one more question about their work was a gift for which I am deeply grateful. I am also indebted to several of Joni's clients—including some who do not appear in this book—who shared their efforts to bring a bit of paradise to their property. Sincere thanks to Abbe and Dennis Sands; Ed Piper and the City of Salinas; the Hewlett-Packard team, especially Steve Shokrai, JoDee DeVries, Phil Koenig, Ted Dukelow, and Kevin Alford; the Dukes; and the staff and landscape volunteers at Elkhorn Slough National Estuarine Research Reserve. Thanks also to Peter Moras, Bruce Stewart, and the staff and volunteers of Return of the Natives.

I received much information and help from many botanic gardens, horticulturists, nursery specialists, ecologists, and botanists around the country. Special thanks to Tom Courtright and his kind and knowledgeable staff at Orchard Nursery & Florist; Rob Gardner at the North Carolina Botanical Garden; Carol Bornstein at the Santa Barbara Botanic Garden; David Fross at Native Sons Nursery; Kim Hawks at Niche Gardens; John Burke at Hines Nurseries; Paul Kephart, formerly of Elkhorn Ranch; Barbara Coe at Suncrest Nurseries; Mel Garber and Mike Dirr at the University of Georgia; John Randall at the Nature Conservancy; and Bruce Butterfield at the National Gardening Association. I am also especially grateful to botanist Al Flinck for discussions about plants, restoration, and good books.

A number of landscape architects provided insight about their profession at various points in this project. Susan Everett at ASLA, the team at Land Ethics, Isabelle Greene, Darrel Morrison, Carol Franklin, Allyson Biskner, the students at Cal Poly San Luis Obispo who allowed me to sit in on their end-of-year presentations, and Walt Tryon deserve special thanks.

Ethan Nosowsky provided sharp-eyed editing, matched by a delightful temperament that made working with him a pleasure. Friends Steve Miller, Sarah Arsone, Deborah Lott, Sarah Price, Shelley Machock, and Susan Milius provided important early encouragement, as did my father, Charles

Phillips, who diligently kept me apprised of weekly radio garden-show topics. Vee Markel kept me informed about gardening challenges in Florida. Thanks to friends Cynthia Lewin, Arthur Fox, Kathy Foley, and Edna Healy for encouragement and warm hospitality during my travels. Thanks also to these and so many other friends, especially Susan Osborne and Lisa Baker, for simply making life enjoyable.

As always, Julie Wilson provided unwavering moral support, for which I am immeasurably thankful.